No Stone Unturned

CRITICAL STUDIES IN THE HEBREW BIBLE

Edited by

Anselm C. Hagedorn
*Humboldt Universität
zu Berlin*

Nathan MacDonald
University of Cambridge

Stuart Weeks
Durham University

No Stone Unturned

Greek Inscriptions
and
Septuagint Vocabulary

James K. Aitken

Winona Lake, Indiana
Eisenbrauns
2014

Library of Congress Cataloging-in-Publication Data

Aitken, J. K. (James Keltie), 1968– author.
  No stone unturned : Greek inscriptions and Septuagint vocabulary /
  James K. Aitken.
      pages   cm — (Critical studies in the Hebrew Bible ; 5)
  Includes bibliographical references and indexes.
  ISBN 978-1-57506-324-9 (pbk. : alk. paper)
  1. Bible. Old Testament. Greek. Septuagint—Criticism,
interpretation, etc.   2. Greek language, Biblical.   I. Title.   II. Series:
Critical studies in the Hebrew Bible ; 5.
      PA710.A37   2014
      487′.4—dc23
                                                    2014037094

Contents

Preface

My interest in the language of the Septuagint has a long history, but the systematic studying of inscriptions and papyri began when I was working at the University of Reading on the project "The Greek Bible in the Graeco-Roman World." There I was inspired by discussions with Tessa Rajak and Sarah Pearce, directors of the project, and Jenny Dines. Their enthusiasm for the study of Hellenistic Judaism and the place of the Greek Bible within it continues to inform my own thinking. The makings of this particular book lie in a presentation I gave on the lexicography of the Septuagint at an international Septuagint meeting in Wuppertal, Germany, in 2006. In presenting the issues of placing the lexicon of the Septuagint within contemporary Greek I realized the value of epigraphic evidence and the extent to which it has been neglected. Thereafter I began to gather systematically data on inscriptions where they offer evidence distinct from the papyri. This book is only a beginning and might perhaps better be seen as a proposal for a research agenda rather than a conclusive discussion.

John Lee has encouraged my work from the beginning, and I am grateful to general discussions with him, as well as Trevor Evans (Macquarie University) and Anne Thompson (University of Cambridge) on matters lexicographic over many years. There is much that they will no doubt disagree with in this volume, but I believe they will support the general principles. In writing this book I have been assisted by a number of people: Rain Robertson read portions of the draft and improved the English immensely, William Ross and Chris Fresch read chapter 3 and offered suggestions from their own experience of working with databases, Malcolm Choat assisted with explanations of certain sigla, and Samuel Blapp and Rain Robertson prompted me on thinking up a title. My thanks go to the editors of the series Critical Studies in the Hebrew Bible, Anselm Hagedorn, Nathan MacDonald, and Stuart Weeks, for enthusiastically accepting the book for publication. Eisenbrauns has been supportive along the way, and I am grateful especially to the excellent assistance of Jim Eisenbraun and Andrew Knapp. As ever, my family has always been supportive of my obscure interests, and I dedicate this to my mother in memory of my father for the years of love and encouragement.

Abbreviations

Symbols used

( )	modern resolution of a symbol or abbreviation
[ ]	lost text (lacuna); the text is supplied by the editor
< >	a mistaken omission by the scribe
{ }	superfluous letter or letters
⟦ ⟧	letter or letters deleted by the scribe in antiquity
\ /	insertion above the line
vac.	"vacat"; indicating that the papyrus is blank at that point
. . .	uncertain reading
|	line break

Other abbreviations

AB	Anchor Bible
ABSA	*Annual of the British School at Athens*
AE	*Archaiologike Ephemeris*
AcOr	*Acta Orientalia*
Ant.	Josephus, *Antiquities of the Jews*
AP	*Anthologia Palatina* (*The Palatine Anthology*)
APIS	The Advanced Papyrological Information System
ArchPap	*Archiv für Papyrusforschung und verwandte Gebiete* (Leipzig; Berlin)
ASAW	Abhandlungen der Sächsischen Akademie der Wissenschaften in Leipzig
BCH	*Bulletin de correspondance hellénique*
BDAG	*A Greek–English Lexicon of the New Testament and Other Early Christian Literature. Based on Walter Bauer's Griechisch-deutsches Wörterbuch zu den Schriften des Neuen Testaments und der frühchristlichen Literatur, sixth edition, ed. Kurt Aland and Barbara Aland, with Viktor Reichmann and on previous English editions by W. F. Arndt, F. W. Gingrich, and F. W. Danker.* Chicago, 2000
BGU	*Ägyptische Urkunden aus den Museen zu Berlin: Griechische Urkunden.* Berlin, 1863–

Bib	*Biblica*
BICS	*Bulletin of the Institute of Classical Studies*
BICSSup	Bulletin of the Institute of Classical Studies Supplements
BIFAO	*Le Bulletin de l'Institut français d'archéologie orientale*
BIOSCS	*Bulletin of the International Organization for Septuagint and Cognate Studies*
BJGS	*Bulletin of Judaeo-Greek Studies*
BJRL	*Bulletin of the John Rylands University Library of Manchester*
BZNW	Beihefte zur Zeitschrift für die neutestamentliche Wissenschaft
CBET	Contributions to Biblical Exegesis and Theology
CBQMS	Catholic Biblical Quarterly Monograph Series
CDD	*The Demotic Dictionary of the Oriental Institute of the University of Chicago (CDD).* Ed. Janet H. Johnson; Chicago [online: oi.uchicago.edu/research/pubs/catalog/cdd/]
ChrEg	*Chronique d'Égypte*
CID	*Corpus des inscriptions de Delphes.* Paris 1977–
CIG	*Corpus inscriptionum Graecarum.* 4 vols.; Berlin, 1825–77
CIRB	*Corpus inscriptionum Regni Bosporani.* Moscow and Leningrad, 1965
DGE	*Diccionario Griego-Español.* Ed. F. R. Adrados; Madrid, 1980–
EA	*Epigraphica Anatolica: Zeitschrift für Epigraphik und historische Geographie Anatoliens*
EDG	R. S. P. Beekes, *Etymological Dictionary of Greek.* 2 vols.; Leiden, 2010
1–2 Esd	1–2 Esdras
Epidoc	Epigraphic Documents in TEI XML [online: http://epidoc.sf.net]
FD	*Fouilles de Delphes. III. Epigraphie.* Paris, 1929
GDI	*Sammlung der griechischen Dialektinschriften.* Ed. H. Collitz, J. Baunack, F. Bechtel et al.; Göttingen, 1884–1915
GELS	T. Muraoka, *A Greek–English Lexicon of the Septuagint.* Leuven, 2009
HALOT	L. Koehler and W. Baumgartner, *Hebrew and Aramaic Lexicon of the Old Testament.* Leiden, 1993
HO	Handbuch der Orientalistik
IAph2007	J. Reynolds, C. Roueché, G. Bodard, *Inscriptions of Aphrodisias* (2007) [online: insaph.kcl.ac.uk/iaph2007]
IBM	*Ancient Greek Inscriptions in the British Museum.* Oxford, 1874–1916
ICKarth	L. Ennabli, *Les Inscriptions funéraires chrétiennes de Carthage.* 3 vols; Collection de l'École française de Rome, 25, 62, 151; Rome, 1975, 1982, 1991

IDelos   *Inscriptions de Délos.* 7 vols.; ed. F. Durrbach, P. Roussel, M. Launey, J. Coupry, and A. Plassart; Paris, 1926–72

IEgVers   E. Bernand, *Inscriptions métriques de l'Égypte gréco-romaine.* Paris, 1969

IEph   *Die Inschriften von Ephesos.* 8 vols. in 9 parts, with a Supplement; Inschriften griechischer Städte aus Kleinasien 11,1–17,4. Bonn, 1979–84

IG   *Inscriptiones Graecae, consilio et auctoritate Academiae Scientarum Berolinensis et Brandenburgensis editaei.* Berlin, 1873–

IGBulg   *Inscriptiones graecae in Bulgaria repertae.* 5 vols.; ed. Georgi Mihailov; Sofia, 1958–70, 1997

IGExtrEast   F. Canali De Rossi, *Iscrizioni dello estremo oriente greco. Un repertorio.* Bonn, 2004

IGLSyria   *Inscriptions grecques et latines de la Syrie, I. Commagène et Cyrrhestique.* Ed. Louis Jalabert and René Mouterde. Paris, 1929–

IGonnoi II   B. Helly, *Gonnoi.* 2 vols; Amsterdam, 1973, vol. 2: *Les Inscriptions*

IKourion   T. B. Mitford, *The Inscriptions of Kourion.* Memoirs of the American Philosophical Society 83; Philadelphia, 1971

IKition   M. Yon et al. *Kition dans les textes. Testimonia littéraires et épigraphiques et Corpus des inscriptions.* Kition-Bamboula V; Paris, 2004

IKnidos   *Die Inschriften von Knidos.* 2 vols.; ed. W. Blümel; Bonn, 1992

IKosHerzog   R. Herzog, *Heilige Gesetze von Kos.* Berlin, 1928

IKret   *Inscriptiones Creticae.* 4 vols.; ed. Margherita Guarducci; Rome, 1935–50

IKyme   H. Engelmann, *Die Inschriften von Kyme.* Bonn, 1976

ILabraunda   J. Crampa, *Labraunda.* Swedish Excavations and Researches III,1–2. *Greek Inscriptions.* 2 vols; Lund, 1969; Stockholm, 1972

IMiletMcCabe   D. F. McCabe, *Miletos Inscriptions. Texts and List.* The Princeton Project on the Inscriptions of Anatolia, The Institute for Advanced Study; Princeton, 1984

IMylasa   W. Blümel, *Die Inschriften von Mylasa,* 1. Inschriften griechischer Städte aus Kleinasien 34. Bonn, 1987

IOlympia   Wilhelm Dittenberger and Karl Purgold, *Die Inschriften von Olympia.* Olympia 5. Berlin, 1896

IPArk   G. Thür and H. Taeuber, *Prozessrechtliche Inschriften der griechischen Poleis: Arkadien (IPArk).* Österreichische Akademie der Wissenschaften. Philosophisch-historische Klasse. Sitzungsberichte [SAW, SbWien] 607. Vienna, 1994

IPerge   S. Şahin, *Die Inschriften von Perge.* 2 vols.; Bonn, 1999–2004

ISardis 7,1	W. H. Buckler and D. M. Robinson. *Sardis*, VII. *Greek and Latin Inscriptions*, Part I. Leiden, 1932
IScM II	I. Stoian, *Inscriptiones Daciae et Scythiae minoris antiquae*. Series altera: Inscriptiones Scythiae minoris graecae et latinae, vol. 2: *Tomis et territorium*. Bucharest, 1987
Isthm.	*The Isthmian odes*
JEA	*The Journal of Egyptian Archaeology*
JIGRE	*Jewish Inscriptions of Graeco-Roman Egypt*. Ed. W. Horbury and D. Noy; Cambridge, 1992
JNSL	*Journal of Northwest Semitic Languages*
JÖAI	*Jahreshefte des Österreichischen Archäologischen Institutes in Wien*
JSOTSup	Journal for the Study of the Old Testament Supplements
JSS	*Journal of Semitic Studies*
JTS	*Journal of Theological Studies*
K–A	*Poetae comici graeci*. 8 vols.; ed. R. Kassel and C. Austin; Berlin, 1983–2001
1–4 Kgdms	1–4 Kingdoms [1–2 Kingdoms = 1–2 Samuel; 3–4 Kingdoms = 1–2 Kings]
KJV	King James Version
LDAB	Leuven Database of Ancient Books
LEH	J. Lust, E. Eynikel, and K. Hauspie, *A Greek–English Lexicon of the Septuagint, Revised Edition*. Stuttgart, 2003
LSJ	*A Greek-English Lexicon*. Ed. H. Liddell, R. Scott, H. S. Jones, and R. McKenzie; 9th ed.; Oxford, 1940
MDAI(A)	Mitteilungen des Deutschen Archaologischen Instituts (Athen.)
Montanari	F. Montanari, *GI – Vocabolario della lingua greca, con la collaborazione di I. Garofalo e D. Manetti*. Turin, 1995
MT	Masoretic Text
NCBC	New Century Bible Commentary
NETS	New English Translation of the Septuagint
NovT	*Novum Testamentum*
OED	*The Oxford English Dictionary*
OG	Old Greek
OGIS	W. Dittenberger, *Orientis Graeci Inscriptiones Selectae*. Leipzig, 1903–5
PAAJR	*Proceedings of the American Academy for Jewish Research*
1–2 Par	1–2 Paralipomena [=1–2 Chronicles]
P.Choach.Survey	P. W. Pestman, *The Archive of the Theban Choachytes*. Leuven, 1993
P.Cair.Zen.	*Zenon Papyri: Catalogue général des antiquités égyptiennes du Musée du Caire*. Ed. C.C. Edgar; Cairo, 1925–40

P.Col.Zen.   *Columbia Papyri*, IV. Ed. W. L. Westermann, C. W. Keyes, and H. Liebesny; New York, 1940

P.Eleph.   *Aegyptische Urkunden aus den Königlichen Museen in Berlin: Griechische Urkunden, Sonderheft. Elephantine-Papyri.* Ed. O. Rubensohn; Berlin, 1907

P.Grenf. I   *An Alexandrian Erotic Fragment and Other Greek Papyri Chiefly Ptolemaic.* Ed. B. P. Grenfell; Oxford, 1896

P.Hamb.   *Griechische Papyrusurkunden der Hamburger Staats- und Universitätsbibliothek.* Leipzig et al., 1911–88

PHI   Packard Humanities Institute

PL   Patrologia Latina

P.Mich.   *Michigan Papyri.* 19 vols; 1931–99

P.Münch.   *Die Papyri der Bayerischen Staatsbibliothek München.* 3 vols.; Stuttgart, 1986

P.Oxy.   *The Oxyrhynchus Papyri.* London, 1898–

P.Petr.   *The Flinders Petrie Papyri.* 3 vols.; Royal Irish Academy, Cunningham Memoirs; Dublin, 1891–1905

P.Rev.   *Revenue Laws of Ptolemy Philadelphus.* Ed. B. P. Grenfell; Oxford, 1896

PSI   *Papiri greci e latini.* 15 vols.; Florence, 1912–2008

P.Tebt.   *The Tebtunis Papyri.* 5 vols.; London, 1902–2005

RB   *Revue biblique*

RBL   *Review of Biblical Literature*

REJ   *Revue des études juives*

Rev.Supplement   *Greek–English Lexicon: Revised Supplement.* Ed. P. G. W. Glare, with the assistance of A. A. Thompson; Oxford, 1996

SB   *Sammelbuch griechischer Urkunden aus Ägypten.* Ed. F. Preisigke et al. 1915–

SBLSCS   Society of Biblical Literature Septuagint and Cognate Studies

SEG   Supplementum Epigraphicum Graecum

SGLG   Sammlung griechischer und lateinischer Grammatiker

Supplement   *Greek–English Lexicon: A Supplement.* Ed. E. A. Barber; Oxford, 1968

Syll.   W. Dittenberger, *Sylloge Inscriptionum Graecarum.* Leipzig, 1915–24

TAM   *Tituli Asiae Minoris.* Vienna, 1901–

TLG   Thesaurus Linguae Graecae

TM   Trismegistos number [online: www.trismegistos.org]

TSAJ   Texte und Studien zum antiken Judentum

UPZ   *Urkunden der Ptolemäerzeit (ältere Funde)* I, *Papyri aus Unterägypten.* Ed. U. Wilcken; Berlin–Leipzig, 1927

VT	*Vetus Testamentum*
VTSup	Vetus Testamentum Supplements
WUNT	Wissenschaftliche Untersuchungen zum Neuen Testament
ZAW	*Zeitschrift für die alttestamentliche Wissenschaft*
ZNW	*Zeitschrift für die neutestamentliche Wissenschaft*
ZPE	*Zeitschrift für Papyrologie und Epigraphik*

CHAPTER I

The Current Study of Septuagint Vocabulary

The evidence we have of any ancient language is typically partial. As there are neither native informants to explain meanings to us nor recorded conversations for us to listen in on, we cannot hear the colloquial or day-to-day expressions of the ancients. The sources we do have are selective, owing to decisions in antiquity as to what to preserve, and fragmentary, owing to the chances of survival. Nonetheless, we are fortunate in the modern era to have access not only to the high literature known to earlier generations of scholars, but also to everyday documents and subliterary papyri that, thanks to discovery and publication in the twentieth century, have opened up the world of the vernacular language. With this in mind, it is imperative to make use of all the data at our disposal when our knowledge is so limited. The expansive publication of new documents has provided us with sources that were previously unknown to researchers but can now be widely consulted and even searched in electronic format. The growth of electronic resources for Greek has enabled far greater possibilities for the researcher, but also placed a greater burden on using the evidence wisely. Indeed, the development of electronic resources "is not just a useful extra for word studies; it means that all available evidence not only can be, but *must* be, used in any work at an advanced level."[1]

Much of this newly accessible evidence still awaits incorporation into dictionaries, and such incorporation will require in some cases reassessment of the entries or at least the inclusion of additional source references. While this task has already begun, inscriptions appear to have particularly been neglected among the sources. This is regrettable given that in the study of biblical Greek the analysis of papyri has had such a major change upon our understanding. Inscriptions could offer yet more advances in our appreciation of the Greek, comparable to the papyri. There are, however,

---

1. J. A. L. Lee, "The Present State of Lexicography of Ancient Greek," in *Biblical Greek Language and Lexicography: Essays in Honor of Frederick W. Danker* (ed. B. Taylor, J. Lee, P. Burton, and R. Whitaker; Grand Rapids, MI: Eerdmans, 2004), 66–74 (67).

1

limitations: the wider geographical distribution of inscriptions across the Mediterranean coupled with their formal language and range of registers might not offer the best comparison for the Egyptian vernacular attested in the Septuagint.[2] Still the distinguishing of inscriptions from papyri affords the opportunity to test the near-exclusive focus on papyri in biblical studies. Inscriptions provide both a broader dataset for comparison with Septuagint vocabulary as well as a different set of language registers for lexicographic research. The fact that the quantity of published inscriptions is close to double the number of papyri also suggests it is a source not to be neglected.[3] Inscriptions are clearly a significant resource for the study of biblical Greek and wider Greek lexicography, and much waits to be discovered.

It is difficult to exaggerate how much outstanding work remains in the lexicography of the Septuagint. In comparison to the study of Classical and New Testament Greek, analysis of the Septuagint vocabulary continues to be an area of research confined to the few. Given the recent publication of lexicographic tools in the field this might seem surprising; yet, in comparison to those available for other areas of Greek they are still few in number and limited in scope. Septuagint vocabulary is distinctive and varied in nature. Some words occur rarely in the language or are only attested after the time of the first Septuagint translations (third to second centuries B.C.E.); others are exclusive to the Septuagint or to literature dependent upon it. Many words will be unfamiliar to those trained only in New Testament Greek, and many will only be known to those who work on documentary sources, but not to those who study classical literature. This is not merely a problem with lack of familiarity for some readers; it is indicative of the time period and nature of Septuagint Greek. Greek of the Hellenistic and Roman periods is not well represented in current reference works, such that the Greek of the Septuagint can sometimes be misleadingly interpreted though evidence from other periods of the language. Accordingly, further primary research is required for a full appreciation of the meaning, register, and lexical history of Septuagint vocabulary. This

---

2. So T. V. Evans, "The Use of Linguistic Criteria for Dating Septuagint Books," *BIOSCS* 43 (2010): 5–22 (12).

3. It has not been possible to calculate how many words are to be found in the databases of inscriptions or papyri. As an indication of their relative sizes, in 2004 when most material was still on CD-ROM without updates, the Duke Databank of Documentary Papyri contained approximately 35,000 documents while the inscriptions (though not as up-to-date as the papyri) had over 60,000. Figures from W. Johnson, "Greek Electronic Resources and the Lexicographical Function," in *Biblical Greek Language and Lexicography: Essays in Honor of Frederick W. Danker* (ed. B. Taylor, J. Lee, P. Burton, and R. Whitaker; Grand Rapids, MI: Eerdmans, 2004), 75–84 (75). Eventually there will be far more papyri than inscriptions, but as yet so much has not been published.

volume is a contribution to that research through focusing on the importance of one neglected source, inscriptions. Its aim is to contribute to the study of Septuagint vocabulary in the first instance and to elucidate some aspects of the meaning, register, syntax, and social context of the words used. By this means we will gain an improved picture of both the translators and their lexical choices. It is also, secondly, a contribution to the history of Greek in drawing together lexical data for a period of the language, and highlighting the use and existence of words.

1. The Septuagint and its vocabulary

It has been well established that the first books of the Septuagint were translated in Egypt in the third century B.C.E. This is implied by the later historical accounts, which, though legendary, may still contain some historical memory.[4] The language and the likely historical setting are stronger indicators of the date and context, and they also point to third-century B.C.E. Egypt.[5] The other Septuagint books were translated over an indeterminate period of time after that. Although little is known of their location and context there is a degree of conformity in their vocabulary and translation technique. It is possible that the first books translated thereafter served as models for the later translations, if one not adhered to rigorously, although it is equally likely that the translators all came from similar "schools" and therefore wrote in a similar style. Its origins as a translated text written in the post-classical period account for some of the peculiarities in its vocabulary and grammar. The distinctiveness of Septuagint vocabulary can easily be illustrated.

(a) Scholarship has established that the vocabulary of the Septuagint for the most part represents the vernacular Greek of the time. Since the end of the nineteenth century, many studies have shown how much this is the case for biblical Greek. Most prominent have been the contributions of Deissmann and his near contemporaries such as Thackeray and Moulton.[6] Apparent new words or rare uses in the Septuagint were found

---

4. While it is true that the *Letter of Aristeas* is largely a fictional literary narrative (B. G. Wright, "The *Letter of Aristeas* and the Question of Septuagint Origins Redux," *Journal of Ancient Judaism* 2 [2011]: 303–25), the broad issues of date and location of the translation therein could be correct.

5. For the date of the third century for the Pentateuch, see J. A. L. Lee, *A Lexical Study of the Septuagint Version of the Pentateuch* (SBLSCS 14; Chico, CA: Scholars Press, 1983), 139–44; T. V. Evans, *Verbal Syntax in the Greek Pentateuch: Natural Greek Usage and Hebrew Interference* (Oxford: Oxford University Press, 2001), 263–64.

6. E.g., G. A. Deissmann, *Bible Studies: Contributions, Chiefly from Papyri and Inscriptions, to the History of the Language, the Literature, and the Religion of Hellenistic Judaism and Primitive Christianity* (Edinburgh: T. & T. Clark, 1909); H. St. J. Thackeray, *A*

to be attested in documentary sources, reflecting the contemporary speech of the time. This accounted for a significant number of words that were not familiar from literary Greek sources but were nevertheless standard Greek of the time. For example, the translators when writing of a 'basket' (κάρταλλος, Deut 26:2, 4; 4 Kgdms 10:7, etc.) or 'cup' (κόνδυ, Gen 44:2, 5, 9, etc.) chose words that can now be seen as common in everyday language of their day. If they wanted to translate the terms for officials, the translators drew upon words used by those around them: 'district governor' (τοπάρχης, Gen 41:34; 4 Kgdms 18:24; Isa 36:9, etc.), 'head foreman' (ἐργοδιώκτης, Exod 3:7; 5:6, 10, etc.), or 'chief wine steward' (ἀρχιοινοχόος, Gen 40:1, 5, 9, etc.). And when faced by difficult theological terms, they could apply in a new context words from the secular sphere: God becomes in the Greek a βοηθός 'helper' (Exod 15:2; 18:4; Deut 33:7) and an ἀντιλήμπτωρ 'protector' (2 Kgdms 22:3; Pss 3:8; 18[17]:3, etc.), terms perhaps first used in appeals to the Ptolemy.[7] Such use of the vernacular means that the Septuagint contains Greek words not attested in classical Greek literature. This arises partly from the translators' preferring words from the vernacular and from the natural change that takes place when words come to replace others by lexical substitution.

(b) A second related phenomenon of Septuagint vocabulary is the extent of so-called "new words" or "neologisms." There appears to be a surprising number of words not attested before the time of the Septuagint or, in a few cases, not attested outside of the Septuagint or the Jewish and Christian literature influenced by it. Such vocabulary has been regularly indicated in Septuagint lexicons. Muraoka provides precise statistics in his *Lexicon* (GELS), informing the reader that there are 9,548 headwords, of which 1,900 are marked by an asterisk—the asterisk indicates that the word is not attested earlier than the Septuagint.[8] Muraoka admits that this does not necessarily mean that those words are created by the translators. He recognizes that an appearance in Polybius (second century B.C.E.), for example, implies the word is simply poorly attested but would have existed

Grammar of the Old Testament in Greek according to the Septuagint, Vol. 1: Introduction, Orthography and Accidence (Cambridge: Cambridge University Press, 1909); J. H. Moulton, *From Egyptian Rubbish-Heaps: Five Popular Lectures on the New Testament* (London: Charles H. Kelly, 1916). See further chapter 2.

7. O. Montevecchi, "Quaedam de graecitate psalmorum cum papyris comparata," in *Proceedings of the IX International Congress of Papyrology. Oslo 19–22 August 1958* (Oslo: Norwegian Universities Press, 1961), 293–310. Reprinted in *Bibbia e papiri: luce dai papiri sulla bibbia greca* (Estudis de papirologia i filologia bíblica 5; Barcelona: Institut de Teologia Fonamental, Seminari de Papirologia, 1999), 97–120.

8. T. Muraoka, *A Greek–English Lexicon of the Septuagint* (Leuven: Peeters, 2009), xiii (GELS).

earlier. Similarly he admits that one must take into account the existence of etymologically or semantically related words, which could imply the word existed but simply has not been preserved in our sources. The *Lexicon* by Lust, Eynikel, and Hauspie (LEH)[9] marks as neologisms ("neol.") those words that seem distinctive to the Septuagint and literature dependent upon it. They also indicate as questionable neologisms ("neol.?") those words not attested before this time but appearing in "contemporary" papyri and literature (again beginning with Polybius in the second century).

Although the editors of these lexicons recognize their suggestions are tentative,[10] the lack of precision over defining such "new words" leads to a distorted picture of Septuagint vocabulary. Taking the crude designations of these lexicons as a starting point suggests that one in five Septuagint words could be a neologism. Such a high percentage cannot be meaningful as it implies an artificial language to an extent unimaginable. The indication of a neologism is merely representative of our limited knowledge of the attestation and should not be taken as a designation of words invented by the translators.[11] When semantic information is the prime concern of a lexicon it may be questioned whether such misleading data should be included in a lexicon at all. It does, nonetheless, helpfully illustrate the extent to which Septuagint vocabulary is not contiguous with classical literature and therefore how much it requires its own investigation. It further justifies how important it is to use all resources at our disposal for elucidating biblical Greek. Inevitably, through the analysis of new data, this study will contribute to a reduction in the number of neologisms in the Septuagint, and will offer examples of where apparent neologisms are in reality attested earlier than Septuagint.

(c) A third typical feature of the Greek of the Septuagint is the presence of new or extended meanings for words already attested in Greek before that time. In earlier scholarship the explanation of a Jewish dialect was commonly invoked to account for these "specialized" meanings.[12]

---

9. J. Lust, E. Eynikel, and K. Hauspie, eds., A *Greek–English Lexicon of the Septuagint, Revised Edition* (Stuttgart: Deutsche Bibelgesellschaft, 2003) (originally published in two parts, 1992, 1996) (LEH).

10. LEH, xiv.

11. See J. K. Aitken, "Neologisms: A Septuagint Problem," in *Interested Readers: Essays on the Hebrew Bible in Honor of David J. A. Clines* (ed. J. K. Aitken, J. M. S. Clines, and C. M. Maier; Atlanta, GA: SBL, 2013), 315–29. It also reflects the lack of precise definition of the broad term "neologism." For the range of categories for neologisms, see D. Xuefu, "Neologismus und Neologismenwörterbuch," in *Wörterbücher in der Diskussion: Vorträge aus dem Heidelberger Lexikographischen Kolloquium* (ed. H. E. Wiegand; Lexicographica. Series maior 27; Tübingen: M. Niemeyer, 1989), 39–73.

12. For scholarship on the concept of "Jewish Greek" and its refutation, see G. H. R. Horsley, "The Fiction of 'Jewish Greek,'" in *New Documents Illustrating Early Christianity,*

Many of these new meanings can now be seen as natural developments in the language and attested in documentary sources of the time.[13] Some, too, can clearly be attributed to interference from the Hebrew source text, and some from the Aramaic in use in Egypt.[14] Such interference from the source text or from the native language of the bilingual speaker is a natural linguistic phenomenon. Nonetheless, decisions on how far interference from the source text is to be seen can only be made once the full scope of the words in Greek has been examined.

Given these features of Septuagint vocabulary, it is a particular task to analyze the words. The resources available for the study of Greek, notably the current lexicons in use, have not been able to keep pace with the speed of publication in documentary sources. Indeed, the dependency of even new works on older lexicons (see below) results in the newer dictionaries not fully incorporating the new material. This is only to be expected, however, as the task of incorporating new material is laborious and can require the rewriting of whole entries. Work already undertaken has been reliant on the main classical Greek lexicons, preeminent among them that of Liddell and Scott. Recognition of the shortcomings in that lexicon will pave the way for identifying the dependency of Septuagint lexicons upon it and their lack of attention to documentary evidence.

2. The tools of Greek lexicography

An enduring problem within lexicography is the reliance shown by the user on the authority of tools.[15] However, although taken as scientific and trustworthy by innocent readers, dictionaries are in reality the summation of the judgments of one scholar or editor. Those judgments may be based upon a compromise, since in the nature of a lexicon a decision must be made and a definition offered, no matter the degree of certainty in the evidence.[16] The dictionary is also dependent upon the knowledge of

---

Volume 5: Linguistic Essays (North Ryde, Australia: Ancient History Documentary Research Centre, Macquarie University, 1989), 5–40.

13. See chapter 2.

14. J. Joosten, "The Septuagint as a Source of Information on Egyptian Aramaic in the Hellenistic Period," in *Aramaic in Its Historical and Linguistic Setting* (ed. H. Gzella and M. L. Folmer; Veröffentlichungen der Orientalistischen Kommission 50; Wiesbaden: Harrassowitz, 2008), 93–105.

15. See on this Lee, "Present State," 66.

16. Cf. J. K. Aitken, "Context of Situation in Biblical Lexica," in *Foundations for Syriac Lexicography III: Colloquia of the International Syriac Language Project* (ed. J. Dyk and W. van Peursen; Perspectives on Syriac Linguistics 4; Piscataway, NJ: Gorgias, 2009), 181–201 (181–82), on the lexicographer as a pragmatist.

the time, the evidence available, or the range of sources the lexicographer chooses to use.

The most influential and important of lexicons in the field has undoubtedly been LSJ. While a work of unsurpassed importance, its weaknesses are readily identifiable and it has been subject to critical review.[17] LSJ (1940), as the ninth edition of Liddell and Scott, has its roots in a lexicon of Classical authors. It thereby derives its meanings from the literature of the Classical era, with some reference to the New Testament. In conception it did not cover the post-classical Koine or documentary sources, even the few that were known in the early nineteenth century. The first edition of Liddell and Scott, published in 1843, was itself a translation and adaptation of Passow's *Handwörterbuch der griechischen Sprache* (1819; 4th ed., 1831).[18] Subsequent editions of Liddell and Scott provided additional references, but these were primarily to obscure authors and, by the time of the ninth edition, to papyri and inscriptions.[19] Since the basis was, however, a lexicon of literature, these additional references merely complicated rather than informed the presentation, as the structure and semantic overview of a word in a lexicon needs to be conceived from the data as a whole. Once a definition has been derived from a selection of occurrences, the introduction of a new set of examples or a new genre can question or nuance the definition. The solution in LSJ was to insert the new references into existing definitions or to include additional sets of definitions, rather than to reconsider the whole entry. Chadwick has shown in detail the problems of the arrangement of LSJ and indicated the scale of the task of rewriting LSJ.[20] References to the Septuagint in LSJ can frequently be found in their own subset of meanings. This reflects the fact that the words were often taken as sharing the meanings of their Hebrew counterparts and therefore provided with distinct senses.[21] It also represents the tendency to add information to LSJ instead of reconsidering the word meanings in light of all the data.

---

17. See, for instance, J. Chadwick, "The Case for Replacing Liddell and Scott," *BICS* 39 (1994): 1–11; J. Chadwick, *Lexicographica graeca: Contributions to the Lexicography of Ancient Greek* (Oxford: Clarendon, 1996); J. Lee, "Releasing Liddell-Scott-Jones from Its Past," in *Classical Dictionaries: Past, Present and Future* (ed. Christopher Stray; London: Duckworth, 2010), 119–38.

18. F. Passow, *Handwörterbuch der griechischen Sprache* (2 vols.; 4th ed.; Leipzig: Vogel, 1831).

19. Chadwick, *Lexicographica graeca*, 3.

20. *Lexicographica graeca*, passim. Cf. Lee, "Present State," 71.

21. The 1925 Preface to Liddell and Scott indicates that A. H. McNeile and A. Llewellyn Davies advised on the LXX material.

A second problem, in addition to the piecemeal gathering of evidence in LSJ, is the reliance on previous lexicons, a topic to which Lee has particularly drawn attention.[22] Not only is the Liddell and Scott tradition dependent on Passow, but Passow itself has its own predecessors that lie behind it. In the process of transmission, definitions are adopted without much reconsideration and sometimes misunderstood, and the source of those definitions is rarely questioned. Modern lexicons find their basis in the vocabularies and thesauri of the Renaissance humanist scholars where they were often aids for translation and were not drawn up by philologists and linguists.[23] Ultimately, most go back to the medieval period, to a time when we have no idea from where the definitions come.[24]

Study of the Septuagint, as we shall see, is built upon these uncertain foundations of earlier Classical lexicons. It is further compounded by the limited lexicographic research on the Greek of the period (Koine) and the lack of lexicographic tools for Koine. This is exacerbated by the wealth of evidence waiting to be explored. The one work recording vocabulary from papyri is Preisigke and Kiessling's *Wörterbuch der griechischen Papyrusurkunden.*[25] As early as 1980 this had been recognised as drastically out of date, and even more so now with continuous publications of papyri proceeding apace.[26] The supplements, too, have not kept up with the publication of material. Its glosses do not arise from lexicographic reconsideration but are standard meanings from other sources. Given the lack of adequate tools for Koine, reliance on older lexicons is revealed to be a problem. Previous lexicons did not have access to the wealth of material published from the late nineteenth century,[27] and therefore their definitions are largely dependent on classical literature. LSJ in its ninth edition had partial access

---

22. J. A. L. Lee, *A History of New Testament Lexicography* (Studies in Biblical Greek 8; New York: Peter Lang, 2003), 6–12, 139–54; Lee, "Present State," 66–68; Lee, "Releasing"; cf. Chadwick, *Lexicographica graeca*, 13.

23. O. A. Piper, "New Testament Lexicography: An Unfinished Task," *Festschrift to Honor F. Wilbur Gingrich: Lexicographer, Scholar, Teacher, and Committed Christian Layman* (ed. E. H. Barth and R. E. Cocroft; Leiden: Brill, 1972), 177–204 (178).

24. Lee, *History*, 51–55.

25. *Wörterbuch der griechischen Papyrusurkunden, mit Einschluss der griechischen Inschriften, Aufschriften, Ostraka, Mumienschilder usw. aus Ägypten* (ed. F. Preisigke and E. Kiessling; 4 vols.; Berlin: Selbstverlag der Erben, 1925–44).

26. Lee, *Lexical Study*, 9. The *Wörterbuch* of Preisigke appeared in 1927, but contained material up to 1921. This was indeed updated by Kiessling in a *Supplement* (1969) with material published between 1940 and 1966, but still remains out of date. The latest *Supplement* (vol. 3; ed. H.-A. Rupprecht and A. Jördens; Wiesbaden: Harrassowitz, 2000) extends to 1988.

27. Cf. A. Passoni Dell'Acqua, "Contributi alla lessicografia dei LXX. I nuovi lessici. In margine a T. Muraoka, *A Greek-English Lexicon of the Septuagint*," *Aegyptus* 74 (1994): 129–35.

to documentary evidence, but was confronted with the already stated difficulty of trying to incorporate it. The supplements to LSJ have aimed to supply more material from documentary sources, but this has not always been collected systematically and certainly has not been able to rectify the preliminary problem with the lexicon. What is required is a full rewriting of entries rather than supplementation.[28]

3. Lexicons of the Septuagint

The tools available for the Septuagint itself are few and far more limited in scope than those available for the New Testament.[29] Until recently, the last extensive and complete Septuagint lexicon was that from the early nineteenth century of J. Schleusner, who also authored a New Testament lexicon.[30] His *Novus thesaurus*, dependent on an earlier work by Biel,[31] is now considerably outdated, appearing as it did before the major publications of Greek papyri and inscriptions. Its lexicographic method is also outdated and problematic for a study of Greek.[32] He analyzed Greek words according to how they translated Hebrew words, and consequently often provided definitions that rely on the meaning of the Hebrew rather

---

28. On the original 1968 Supplement, see J. A. L. Lee, "A Note on Septuagint Material in the Supplement to Liddell and Scott," *Glotta* 47 (1969): 234–42; Chadwick, "Case for Replacing," 7–10; K. Hauspie, "The LXX Quotations in the LSJ Supplements of 1968 and 1996," in *Biblical Greek Language and Lexicography: Essays in Honor of Frederick W. Danker* (ed. B. Taylor, J. Lee, P. Burton, and R. Whitaker; Grand Rapids, MI: Eerdmans, 2004), 108–25. See too J. K. Aitken, "Σχοῖνος in the Septuagint," *VT* 50 (2000): 433–44, for the problems of Septuagint material in the Supplements.

29. This applies as much to grammars as to lexicons. For a brief survey of lexicographic tools to the Septuagint, see E. Tov, "Some Thoughts on a Lexicon of a Septuagint," in *The Greek and Hebrew Bible: Collected Essays on the Septuagint* (Leiden: Brill, 1999), 95–108 (97–98) (originally published: *BIOSCS* 9 [1976], 14–46). Cf. R. A. Kraft, ed., *Septuagintal Lexicography* (SBLSCS 1; Missoula, MT: Society of Biblical Literature, 1972).

30. J. F. Schleusner, *Novus thesaurus philologico-criticus, sive lexicon in LXX et reliquos interpretes graecos ac scriptores apocryphos Veteris Testamenti* (5 vols.; Leipzig: in libraria Weidmannia, 1820–21); *Novum Lexicon graeco-latinum in Novum Testamentum: congessit et variis observationibus philologicis illustravit* (2 vols.; Lepizig: in officina Weidmanniana, 1792).

31. J. C. Biel, *Novus Thesaurus Philologicus, sive lexicon in LXX et alios interpretes et scriptores apocryphos Veteris Testamenti* (3 vols.; Den Haag: Bouvink, 1779–81). We may also note G. Ewing, *A Greek Grammar, and Greek and English Scripture Lexicon Containing All the Words which Occur in the Septuagint and Apocrypha, as Well as in the New Testament* (2nd ed.; Glasgow: J. Hedderwick for A. Constable, 1812), which is more of a glossary than a descriptive lexicon (the first edition of 1801, "a compendious lexicon, for the use of those who wish to make themselves acquainted with the New Testament in the original," does not seem to have included the Septuagint). Tov, "Some Thoughts," 97, also mentions a glossary by Rosenarch (1642).

32. On the history of this Septuagint lexicon, with criticisms of its method, see J. Lust, "J. F. Schleusner and the Lexicon of the Septuagint," *ZAW* 102 (1990): 256–62.

than the Greek words in context. Nevertheless, there is a great deal of information provided, including discussion of many occurrences, even in the Three (Aquila, Theodotion, and Symmachus).[33] In comparison to more recent lexicons, it does have some benefits. It incorporates, to a far greater degree than many, analysis of the occurrences, discussions of meanings in particular contexts, and related data such as variants and patristic citations.

The recent lexicon by Lust, Eynikel, and Hauspie (LEH) was a major achievement in being the first and only complete lexicon since Schleusner, providing an up-to-date bibliography and drawing upon recent research.[34] Its scope is very limited, nonetheless, citing only the first five attestations of a given meaning for a word rather than the most illustrative examples. It also does not provide full entries for frequently occurring words (especially particles and conjunctions). In many instances its most serious defect is its reliance on LSJ for its meanings. All lexicons are to some degree dependent on their predecessors, as noted above, but the citation of Septuagint material in LSJ is particularly problematic. It therefore serves as an unfortunate basis for a Septuagint lexicon.[35]

Muraoka's *Lexicon*, now complete, is a major advance on its predecessors because his aim has been to analyze each lexeme in context, as a proper lexicographic approach should. As to how far one should take into account the influence of the source languages remains a controversial question in Septuagint lexicography.[36] Muraoka does not ignore the likely Hebrew *Vorlage*, paying some attention to it, as is required in Septuagint study, but he focuses more on the meaning from the context.[37] As far as possible it is a fresh analysis not dependent on previous lexicons, although the definitions do often coincide with those of predecessors. He judiciously includes bibliographic items where they have informed the presentation

---

33. For some of the benefits in still consulting Schleusner, see F. A. Gosling, "The Inaccessible Lexicon of J. F. Schleusner," *JNSL* 26 (2000): 19–31.

34. Excluded from this discussion are F. Rehkopf, *Septuaginta-Vokabular* (Göttingen: Vandenhoeck & Ruprecht, 1989), which is little more than a vocabulary list, and B. A. Taylor, *The Analytical Lexicon to the Septuagint: A Complete Parsing Guide* (Grand Rapids, MI: Zondervan, 1994), which parses all the words but does not provide definitions. A new second edition of *The Analytical Lexicon* (2010) does now include definitions, but these are taken from LEH.

35. See, e.g., G. B. Caird, "Towards a Lexicon of the Septuagint, I, II," *JTS* 19 (1968): 453–75; 20 (1969): 21–40; Lee, "Present State," 70.

36. Earlier intermediary versions of the *Lexicon* were published in 1993 and 2002. For criticism of taking words as they appear in context, see J. Lust, "Two New Lexica of the Septuagint and Related Examples," *JNSL* 19 (1993): 95–105.

37. It is notable that in the final version, Muraoka has dispensed with giving the Hebrew equivalents at the end of each entry, but has instead published them in a separate volume: T. Muraoka, *A Greek–Hebrew/Aramaic Two-Way Index to the Septuagint* (Leuven: Peeters, 2010).

of an entry, but not if they present a contrary view. As far as documentary and Koine evidence is concerned, Muraoka takes into consideration the meaning of words in non-biblical Greek, although this is inconsistent and dependent more on literary than documentary sources.[38] It does not serve as a comprehensive survey of the words in contemporary Koine, and certainly does not reflect the comprehensive offering of the Bauer lexicographic tradition.[39] It is therefore valuable as an analysis of the words in context, but does not place the words within the language of the time.

A new project currently underway is the *Historical and Theological Lexicon of the Septuagint*, under the editorship of E. Bons and J. Joosten.[40] Their aim is to present, in four volumes, significant words in the Septuagint and place them within the history of the language. Thus, the *Lexicon* will provide data on the earlier Classical usage of the word, its use in papyri and inscriptions, and its use in Jewish and early patristic sources. It will establish a basis for further work in this area, although it remains to be seen how far the documentary material will be examined and the extent to which it will inform the discussion.

4. Septuagint lexicons and their predecessors

As an illustration of the reliance of Septuagint lexicons on their predecessors, a few small examples have been chosen. In some cases the adoption of the glosses in modern translations of the Septuagint represents the influence of these lexicons on users.

4.a. Antiquated language

Dependency can easily be seen in cases where the same glosses are offered, especially when those glosses contain outdated language. The first edition of Liddell and Scott was published in 1843, meaning its glosses were written in the English of Victorian England and which now require

---

38. F. Shaw in "Review of T. Muraoka, *A Greek–English Lexicon of the Septuagint*," *Bryn Mawr Classical Review* 2010-04-20 [online: bmcr.brynmawr.edu/2010/2010-04-20.html], calculates that in the first 25 pages of the lexicon (covering 370 lemmata) there are only four citations of ancient sources.

39. The latest in the Bauer series is a revision by F. W. Danker, *A Greek–English Lexicon of the New Testament and Other Early Christian Literature* (3rd ed.; Chicago: University of Chicago Press, 2001) (BDAG).

40. See J. Joosten, "The Historical and Theological Lexicon of the Septuagint: A Sample Entry—εὐλογέω," in *XIV Congress of the IOSCS, Helsinki, 2010* (ed. M. K. H. Peters; SBLSCS 59; Atlanta, GA: SBL, 2013), 347–55; E. Bons and A. Passoni Dell'Acqua, "A Sample Article: κτίζω – κτίσις – κτίσμα – κτίστης," in *Septuagint Vocabulary: Pre-History, Usage, Reception* (ed. E. Bons and J. Joosten; SBLSCS 58; Atlanta, GA: SBL, 2011), 173–88.

some updating. Thus the choice of the antiquated 'supperless' (LEH 9: 'without the evening meal, supperless') for ἄδειπνος (Dan 6:18) reflects the influence of LSJ (20: 'without the evening meal, supperless'). It has wisely been dropped by GELS ('without the evening meal'), which none-theless shows the influence of LSJ in preserving the first of the translation options.[41] In the context of Daniel a simple translation 'without eating' or perhaps 'without dinner' would be sufficient. Conversely, for ἁλυσιδωτός GELS (30) merely repeats the LSJ definition 'wrought in chain fashion' (LSJ 74). This is despite the archaic use of 'fashion' here, which is diffi-cult to interpret but probably denotes either 'a particular shape, style, or pattern'[42] or the style of dress. LEH (30) seeks to update the definition but misunderstands the English, interpreting fashion to denote 'manner, mode, way' and giving us 'wrought in chain manner, like a chain.' As a result, someone dressed in a 'chainmail breastplate' (ἁλυσιδωτός θώραξ; 3 Kdgms 17:5; Polybius 6.23.15) would only be in 'a breastplate like a chain.' Naturally the translations do not follow this option.

4.b. Misreadings

Misreading can also arise from the density of the information pre-sented on the page of a lexicon. Thus, LSJ (54) explains ἄκρατος as denot-ing '*unmixed, neat*, esp. of wine,' but LEH raises the alcohol content by defining it as 'unmixed, very strong (of wine)' (23). It appears that the su-perlative 'very' comes from a gloss further on in the LSJ entry: 'οἶνος πάνυ ἄ. very *strong*, X.*An*.4.5.27.' The use of the italics is crucial in this case, as it indicates that the headword is to be translated as 'strong,' and the adverb 'very' is from the word πάνυ in the passage of Xenophon.

4.c. Adoption into translation

Mere adoption of a previous lexicon's gloss may also belie problems in the glosses or definitions. A harmless rendering is LSJ's translation of εὐ(ε)ίλατος as 'very merciful' (717), this time including the adverb 'very' within its gloss. There is no accounting for the superlative adverb, however, other than as an attempt to render the prefix εὐ- and thereby to account for each element in the Greek. 'Merciful' would be sufficient as a transla-tion, especially when there is no evidence to suggest that someone who was εὐ(ε)ίλατος was more merciful than someone who was ἵλαος. Nonethe-less, GELS (30) repeats the gloss 'very merciful' while LEH (250) reduces

---

41. NETS (1011) translates the expression as 'without supper,' which equally sounds archaic in English and probably is under the influence of LSJ or LEH.

42. Classed as "somewhat archaic" by the OED.

it to the simple 'merciful.' The superlative 'very merciful' reappears in the NETS translation in both instances of the word (Ps 98[99]:8; 1 Esd 8:53).

4.d. A long prehistory

Finally, the dependency can have a longer history than just that of the modern lexicons on LSJ. The noun θῖβις is an Egyptian loanword in Greek and appears in Exodus as the translation of the object (Hebrew תבה) into which Moses was placed (Exod 2:3, 5, 6). An Egyptian flavor is imparted by the translator to the passage by this means, and a phonetic matching to the Hebrew equivalent תבה 'ark.' The translator did not choose the alternative equivalent of κιβωτός, preferred by the Genesis translator for Noah's ark (תבה) and by the translator of the tabernacle account for the ark (Hebrew ארון) of the covenant. GELS (330) has followed LSJ with its rendering for θῖβις of '*basket* plaited from papyrus' (LSJ 801), while LEH (276) only takes the italicized part 'basket.' Remarkably, the rendering of LSJ can be found as early as the ninth century when we find the definition in the Συναγωγή of an anonymous lexicographer, and afterwards in Photius and in the tenth-century Suda:

θῖβις· κιβώτιον ἐκ βύβλου πλεκτόν, ὡς κοφινῶδες

θίβις: a box plaited from papyrus, like a basket[43]

It may be surmised that the influence of the Suda upon later lexicographers led Liddell and Scott to choose this definition and to translate, it appears, ἐκ βύβλου πλεκτόν literally. While it is conceivable that the definition is correct, it does not give confidence in the lexicons that repeat it without further consideration. How these lexicons came up with their definition may be lost, but the original source seems to be Josephus, who recounts that Moses' family made for him a πλέγμα βίβλινον ἐμφερὲς τῇ κατασκευῇ κοιτίδι "wicker-work made of papyrus, similar in shape to a basket" (*Ant.* 2.220).[44] Oddly, later, in a story unique to Josephus, Moses himself makes πλέγματα . . . ἐμφερῆ κιβωτοῖς ἐκ βίβλου "baskets . . . made of papyrus, similar to chests" (*Ant.* 2.246), where Josephus compares the baskets to κιβωτός, the translation equivalent for an 'ark.' There is no extant church father known to the present author who interprets Exodus in a similar way to Josephus, but the influence of this reading can be seen even in iconographic tradition up to the present day. The adoption of such an ancient

---

43. I. C. Cunningham, *Synagoge:* Συναγωγὴ λέξεων χρησίμων (SGLG 10; Berlin: de Gruyter, 2003). Cf. Hesychius who defines it as πλεκτόντι.

44. Translation of L. H. Feldman, *Judean Antiquities 1–4: Translation and Commentary* (Leiden: Brill, 2004), 194.

interpretation without fresh analysis raises suspicion over the definition 'basket' and especially one 'plaited from papyrus.'

Documentary evidence assists in reconsidering the noun θῖβις. The Demotic word *tby*, as its Middle Egyptian ancestor, denotes a 'chest' or 'box,' and the Hebrew *Vorlage* of the Greek translation likewise would ordinarily mean the same.[45] Therefore, there is a case to reconsider the meaning of θίβις especially when, in the Greek version of this passage, it is not indicated that it is made of papyrus—that is only in the Hebrew and has been omitted by the translation. Loanwords can nonetheless develop new senses in their adopted language such that resorting to the original language is only one clue. The solution is to examine its uses in contemporary Greek, and here we must resort to documentary papyri as there are no literary uses. Unfortunately the examples are very few and do not offer definitive results. In one, the noun appears merely as an item in a list of goods handed over by a commercial agent (P.Cair.Zen. 1.59069.5 [TM 725]; 257 B.C.E.), but in another third-century papyrus the writer recounts how he entered the treasury (τα]μιεῖον) and found some money in a θίβις:

εὑρεῖν | ὅτι ἐν τῆι θίβει ⟦εν⟧ εἴη τὸ ἀργύριον

to find that there was money in the *thibis* (P.Petr. 3.51.3–4 [TM 7466])

It is tempting to conclude that this is a money chest rather than a basket, but no certain conclusions can be drawn from this example. There remain further questions to explore even with this one small word, including the possibility of alternative etymologies[46] and the meaning of an Aramaic cognate.[47] At the least, it has been shown that heritage of the translation '*basket* plaited from papyrus' is not a certain indicator of the meaning when its roots lie as far back as Josephus in a paraphrastic history. When there is documentary evidence to hand, to rely on one's predecessors is to miss an opportunity for providing the full picture of the word's meaning.

In all the lexicons discussed here the limitation of the corpus to a select body of literature, rather than examination of the words within the

---

45. See *The Demotic Dictionary of the Oriental Institute of the University of Chicago (CDD)* (ed. J. H. Johnson; Chicago: Oriental Institute), T: 138–39 [Online: oi.uchicago.edu/research/pubs/catalog/cdd/]. Discussion in B. H. Stricker, "Trois études de phonétique et de morphologie coptes," *AcOr* 15 (1937): 1–20 (18); P. Grelot, "Études sur les textes araméens d'Éléphantine," *RB* 78 (1971): 515–44 (519).

46. See *EDG* 1: 548–49.

47. Note that J. Hoftijzer and K. Jongeling (*Dictionary of the North-West Semitic Inscriptions* [2 vols.; HO 21; Leiden: Brill, 1995], 1202) suggest that Old Aramaic *tb* means 'basket.'

history of Greek, is necessary for a project ever to be finished. It does, however, restrict the lexicographic value of the data. The Septuagint lexicons' reliance on their predecessors, especially LSJ, and the lack of attention to the documentary sources prevent a fresh analysis of the data. As a result, examination of the Septuagint in the light of contemporary Greek should be the way forward.

CHAPTER 2

Documentary Evidence in Biblical Lexicography

In 257 B.C.E., Toubias sent a eunuch and four young slave boys as personal gifts to Apollonios and Ptolemy to mark their mutual standing. As Toubias's scribe sat down to write out the inventory, he listed the features of the fourth boy:

τρογγυλοπρόσωπος ἔσσιμος γλαυκὸς πυρράκης τετανὸς οὐλὴ ἐμ μετώπωι

Round face. Nose flat. Gray eyes. Fiery complexion. Long straight hair.[1]

Little did he realize that when he described the 'fiery' or 'ruddy' complexion as πυρράκης, he was leaving vital evidence to be unearthed some 2000 years later. Until the discovery of papyri in the nineteenth century, the word πυρράκης was only known from the Septuagint (Gen 25:25; 1 Kgdms 16:12; 17:42), describing the striking appearance of both Esau and David. It appeared to be uniquely biblical as it was not attested in Greek literary sources. Now, with the discovery of the papyrus letter,[2] it could be seen as a common word in unflattering descriptions, a world away from the portrayal of heroic characteristics in literature. This word is just one of countless traces left by unnamed scribes of non-literary language that illuminate our understanding of biblical Greek. Without them it would have been easier to suggest that the Septuagint translators were inventing words or using their own distinct dialect.

1. The role of papyri

The importance of papyri in understanding biblical Greek was recognized early in the nineteenth century,[3] but it has been slow to exert

---

1. P.Cair.Zen. 1.59076.IV.9–12 (TM 731). Translation from R. S. Bagnall and P. Derow, *The Hellenistic Period: Historical Sources in Translation* (Blackwell Sourcebooks in Ancient History 1; Oxford: Blackwell, 2004), 113.

2. The adjective is now found in seven papyri of the third to second centuries B.C.E.

3. E.g., H. G. J. Thiersch, *De Pentateuchi versione Alexandrina: libri tres* (Erlangae: apud Theod. Blaesing, 1841), 87–90.

the influence it should. To a large extent these sources offered the sort of vocabulary not attested in the literature known up to that point, reflecting as they do the contemporary language without the refinement of the literature. Early editors of the papyri were often aware of this and made comparison with Septuagint or New Testament words in their editions.[4] Comparison between papyri and biblical Greek is most associated with the name Adolf Deissmann, who made recourse to documentary evidence, particularly but not exclusively papyri.[5] Consequently, biblical Greek was shown not to be a peculiar Jewish dialect or sacred language, but, for the most part, standard Greek of the time. Deissmann more than any before him recognized the importance of the evidence from both inscriptions and papyri that were being published in his lifetime:

> Every one of the minute peculiarities distinguishing the text of the Bible from that of Plato and Xenophon is found in the contemporary Greek of the lingua franca as evidenced in the inscriptions, ostraca, and particularly the papyri now in hand.[6]

He showed how idioms that seemed to be Semitic were in fact attested in contemporary Greek and how apparently new words in biblical Greek were in fact already known at the time.[7] The language was not to be seen as a particular form of Greek but was typical of the vernacular used in Egypt in Ptolemaic times.

---

4. E.g., J. P. Mahaffy, *The Flinders Petrie Papyri: With Transcriptions, Commentaries and Index* (3 vols.; Dublin: Academy House, 1893), 2: 46, on εὐείλατος; B. P. Grenfell, *An Alexandrian Erotic Fragment and other Greek Papyri Chiefly Ptolemaic* (Oxford: Clarendon, 1896), 34, on θίβη/θίβις.

5. See, in particular for the Septuagint, G. A. Deissmann, *Bibelstudien* (Marburg: N. G. Elwert, 1895); and *Neue Bibelstudien* (Marburg: N. G. Elwert, 1897). The two volumes were translated as *Bible Studies* (Edinburgh: T. & T. Clark, 1909). For a summary of his position, see G. A. Deissmann, "Hellenistisches Griechisch," in *Realencyklopädie für protestantische Theologie und Kirche* (ed. A. Hauk; 24 vols.; 3rd ed.; Leipzig: Hinrich, 1896–1913), 7: 627–39. For a recent study of Deissmann's life and academic biography, see A. Gerber, *Deissmann the Philologist* (BZNW 171; Berlin: de Gruyter, 2010). One thing Gerber traces is the immense time Deissmann spent excavating and engaging with epigraphic sources *in situ*.

6. "Hellenistic Greek," *The New Schaff-Herzog Encyclopedia of Religious Knowledge* (ed. Samuel Macauley Jackson; 12 vols.; New York: Funk and Wagnalls, 1908–12), 5: 211–15 (213). It is an abridged English version of the article published in the *Realencyklopädie*. A more literal and unabridged English version of the original German article has been published as "Hellenistic Greek with Special Consideration of the Greek Bible," in *The Language of the New Testament: Classic Essays* (ed. S. Porter; Sheffield: JSOT, 1991), 39–59.

7. Deissmann has sometimes been criticized on a number of counts, but he equally has been defended. For a presentation of views, see M. Silva, "Bilingualism and the Character of Palestinian Greek," *Bib* 61 (1980): 198–219.

Deissmann, for example, was the first to identify ἀντιλήμπτωρ in papyri as having significance for biblical Greek.[8] He noted how the word had not hitherto been authenticated outside biblical literature and had therefore been seen as "peculiar to the LXX." Given that there are now nine attestations in documentary papyri (the earliest being from Memphis; UPZ 1.14r2.18 [TM 3405]; 158 B.C.E.), and a number of later examples in Christian inscriptions (e.g., SEG 34:1668, B 2), this word is representative of the remarkable increase in the past century of examples from which we might draw. However, the consequences are more than disproving the view of Jewish Greek,[9] and the data from documentary sources inform our understanding of a range of nuances and connotations of the words. In the case of ἀντιλήμπτωρ we see how a term used in the Ptolemaic court and of the divine Ptolemies themselves is adopted as a term for God in the Psalms.[10]

Studies prior to Deissmann had already explained the meaning of Septuagint vocabulary in the light of contemporary evidence,[11] and occasionally used it to confirm an Egyptian setting for some of the translations.[12] It was soon utilized in an array of grammatical studies to account for morphological and syntactic features.[13] As publication of the sources continued, further studies assisted in explaining some of the surprising terminology in the Septuagint,[14] although these have remained the minority in Septuagint studies throughout the twentieth century.[15] The foundation laid by Deissmann and his contemporaries was built upon by O. Montevecchi and J. Lee.[16] Lee in particular, and in the face of a renewed interest in the concept of a Jewish Greek, sought to explain once more the place of

8. Deissmann, *Bible Studies*, 91; cf. O. Montevecchi, "Quaedam de graecitate psalmorum cum papyris comparata," reprinted in *Bibbia e papiri. Luce dai papiri sulla Bibbia greca*, a cura di A. Passoni Dell'Acqua (Estudios de Papirologia y Filologia Biblica 5; Barcelona: Institut de Teologia fondamental, Seminari de papirologia, 1999), 97–120 (106).

9. See especially G. H. R. Horsley, "The Fiction of 'Jewish Greek'," in *New Documents Illustrating Early Christianity, Volume 5: Linguistic Essays* (North Ryde, Australia: Ancient History Documentary Research Centre, Macquarie University, 1989), 5–40.

10. Deissmann, *Bible Studies*, 91–92.

11. E.g., J. E. I. Walch, *Observationes in Matthaeum ex graecis inscriptionibus* (Jena, 1779); B. Jacob, "Das Buch Esther bei den LXX," *ZAW* 10 (1890): 280–90.

12. E.g., Jacob, "Buch Esther," 289–90.

13. E.g., H. St. J. Thackeray, *A Grammar of the Old Testament in Greek according to the Septuagint* (Cambridge: Cambridge University Press, 1909).

14. E.g., R. M. Gwynn, "Notes on the Vocabulary of Ecclesiastes in Greek," *Hermathena* 42 (1920): 115–22.

15. Cf. J. A. L. Lee, "*A Lexical Study* Thirty Years On, with Observations on 'Order' Words in the LXX Pentateuch," in *Emanuel: Studies in Hebrew Bible, Septuagint and Dead Sea Scrolls in Honor of Emanuel Tov* (ed. S. M. Paul, R. A. Kraft, L. H. Schiffman, and W. W. Fields; VTSup 94; Leiden: Brill, 2003), 513–24 (516).

16. Montevecchi's writings have been collected together in Montevecchi, *Bibbia e papiri* (1999); J. A. L. Lee, *A Lexical Study of the Septuagint Version of the Pentateuch* (SBLSCS, 14; Chico, CA: Scholars Press, 1983).

the Septuagint within Koine.[17] Other smaller studies have also contributed to this picture,[18] some devoted to specific lexicographic issues,[19] and others to the broader social significance.[20] In a retrospective on his work Lee admits that there has been little significant advance in using papyri since his *Lexical Study* of 1980. There have been no major studies examining the data from papyri, and the lexicons that have appeared have not undertaken fresh analysis of documentary sources.[21] Nonetheless, there are signs that a new generation will take this agenda on, although the difficulties working with the material might still inhibit further research. Bons and Joosten's *Historical and Theological Lexicon*, discussed in chapter 1, will provide a foundation for future research as well as encourage those scholars writing the entries to take this material into account. At the same time, studies of the papyrological evidence are appearing steadily.[22]

Whereas New Testament studies have been furnished with a Bauer lexicon (BDAG) that documents carefully the extrabiblical sources, and documentary evidence is explicitly employed in Moulton and Milligan's

17. See G. H. R. Horsley, "*Res Bibliographicae*: Divergent Views on the Nature of the Greek of the Bible," *Bib* 65 (1984): 393–403; Horsley, "Fiction of 'Jewish Greek'; cf. Lee, "*A Lexical Study* Thirty Years On," 513.

18. E.g., A. Passoni Dell'Acqua, "La terminologia dei reati nei προστάγματα dei Tolemei e nella versione dei LXX," in *Proceedings of the XVIIIth International Congress of Papyrology, Athens 25–31 May 1986* (ed. B. G. Mandilaras; 2 vols.; Athens: Greek Papyrological Society, 1988), 2: 335–50; A. Passoni Dell'Acqua, "Il Pentateuco dei LXX testimone di istituzioni di età tolemaica," *Annali di Scienze religiose* 4 (1999): 171–200; H. Cadell, "Vocabulaire de la législation ptolémaïque. Problème du sens de *dikaióma* dans le Pentateuque," in Κατὰ τοὺς Ο′. *"Selon les Septante": Trente études sur la Bible grecque des Septante. En hommage à Marguerite Harl* (ed. G. Dorival and O. Munnich; Paris: Cerf, 1995), 207–21.

19. E.g., F. Vattioni, "La lessicografia dei LXX nei papiri," *Studia Papyrologica* 19 (1980): 39–59.

20. H. Heinen, "Zur Terminologie der Sklaverei im ptolemäischen Ägypten: παῖς und παιδίσκη in den Papyri und der Septuaginta," in *Atti del XVII Congresso internazionale di papirologia* (3 vols.; Naples: Centro Internazionale per lo Studio dei Papiri Ercolanesi, 1984), 3: 1287–95; B. G. Wright, "Δοῦλος and Παῖς as Translations of עבד: Lexical Equivalences and Conceptual Transformations," in *IX Congress of the International Organization for Septuagint and Cognate Studies. Cambridge, 1995* (ed. B. A. Taylor; SBLSCS 45; Atlanta, GA: Scholars, 1997), 263–77.

21. Lee, "*A Lexical Study* Thirty Years On," 516.

22. E.g., J. K. Aitken, "Phonological Phenomena in Greek Papyri and Inscriptions and Their Significance for the Septuagint," in *Studies in the Greek Bible: Essays in Honor of Francis T. Gignac, S.J.* (ed. J. Corley and V. Skemp; CBQMS 44; Washington, DC: The Catholic Biblical Association of America, 2008), 256–77. M. N. van der Meer, "Trendy Translations in the Septuagint of Isaiah: A Study of the Vocabulary of the Greek Isaiah 3,18–23 in the Light of Contemporary Sources," in *Die Septuaginta—Texte, Kontexte, Lebenswelten. Internationale Fachtagung veranstaltet von Septuaginta Deutsch (LXX.D), Wuppertal 20.–23. Juli 2006* (ed. M. Karrer und W. Kraus; Tübingen: Mohr Siebeck, 2008), 581–96; M. N. van der Meer, "Problems and Perspectives in Septuagint Lexicography: The Case of Non-Compliance (ΑΠΕΙΘΕΩ)," in *Septuagint Vocabulary: Pre-History, Usage, Reception* (ed. J. Joosten and E. Bons; Atlanta, GA: SBL, 2011), 65–86.

resource for the New Testament,[23] there is no equivalent for Septuagint Greek. This is all the more regrettable when it is realized that the relation between Septuagint and New Testament Greek is not as close as might be expected.[24] Contemporary documentary material has not been exploited more in biblical studies owing to the difficulties in examining Koine sources. There are few reference works that can be consulted, but without adequate indices, lexicons, or concordances, it is difficult for the scholar to keep abreast of new publications. There has been an exponential growth in data since the time of Deissmann and new publications, including new discoveries, are continually appearing.[25]

New Testament studies continue to take only sporadic interest in papyrological sources, although individual studies or volumes dealing with the relation between New Testament and papyri have occasionally appeared.[26] Their scope, however, tends to cover more than lexicography.[27]

2. Inscriptions and biblical lexicography

Greek inscriptions shed light on every aspect of ancient life from a wide geographical spread. As evidence of Greek writing on solid material, whether stone, bone, rock, or wood, inscriptions have survived in places where the more perishable papyri have not. Surveying them is a veritable tour of the ancient world. They take us from as far east as Kandahar in modern Afghanistan, across Mesopotamia and the Levant, down into the Persian Gulf and up to the northern shore of the Black Sea, west to Spain and ancient Gaul, and south again into north Africa. In some cases inscriptions from these regions provide the best if not the only witnesses to languages in that geographical area. They also reflect large dialectal variation in the classical period, a variation that is diminished by the Koine but not completely obliterated (see chapter 6).

---

23. J. H. Moulton and G. Milligan, *The Vocabulary of the Greek Testament, Illustrated from the Papyri and other Non-Literary Sources* (London: Hodder & Stoughton, 1930). Originally issued in eight parts from 1914–1929.

24. Lee, *Lexical Study of the Septuagint*, 9.

25. Aitken, "Phonological Phenomena," 259–61.

26. A good recent example is G. B. Bazzana, "New Testament Studies and Documentary Papyri: Interactions and New Perspectives," *Papyrologica Lupiensia* 22 (2013): 5–34. E. A. Mathieson provides more of a survey of possibilities combined with a detailed reading of one papyrus as illustration ("The Language of the Gospels: Evidence from the Inscriptions and the Papyri," in *The Content and the Setting of the Gospel Tradition* [ed. M. Harding and A. Nobbs; Grand Rapids, MI: Eerdmans, 2010], 62–78).

27. E.g., P. Arzt-Grabner and C. M. Kreinecker, eds., *Light from the East: papyrologische Kommentare zum Neuen Testament: Akten des internationalen Symposions vom 3.–4. Dezember 2009 am Fachbereich Bibelwissenschaft und Kirchengeschichte der Universität Salzburg* (Wiesbaden: Harrassowitz, 2010).

Greek inscriptions begin to appear with the writing of Greek letters in the eighth century B.C.E. (five centuries earlier than our first papyri) and continue into the Byzantine Empire. One of the first is the famous "Nestor's cup," a brief but charming introduction to the language from near Naples. The inscription scratched on the side of a cup opens with a declaration in verse of its owner: "Of Nestor am I, a cup pleasant to drink from."[28] Many inscriptions are short in such fashion, being markings on cups, jars, or vases, graffiti on walls, jottings on ostraca, or brief dedications at shrines. Most well known are probably the many, and often long, political decrees and record lists of elections, often written in a formal style and using generic terms. The large numbers of these from Attica, given the political importance of Athens and its regions in the fifth and fourth centuries, have provided a corpus of sufficient size to be worthy of corpus-based linguistic studies. Most studies of epigraphic language have accordingly been of Attic inscriptions.[29] Legal texts are also in abundance, including sacred laws specifying the governance of shrines (see chap. 4 §12).

Other inscriptions provide us with a variety of literary evidence, some coming close to literature known from literary papyri. These could be short poems such as that left by a pensive individual in a toilet of Ephesus (see chap. 5 §3c), the historical chronicle from the island of Paros (IG XII 5.444; see chap. 4 §16), or the extensive musings of the Epicurean Diogenes carved on a wall in the town of Oenoanda in southern Asia Minor.[30] Most important of all for Septuagint studies are the surprising number of religious texts, whether the hymns to Isis or Serapis (see chap. 6 §4) or the rare Greek Buddhist texts from Kandahar (see IGExtrEast 292; chapter 4). As publications of inscriptions continue every year it is not possible to put a figure on the number in print already. An indication of the scale of the evidence can be gleaned from Millar, who estimated in 1983 the total number of Greek and Latin inscriptions to be in the region of half a million or more, with Greek serving the larger proportion of that estimate.[31] The published editions of inscriptions vary. Some appear in a regular series such as the *Inscriptiones Graecae* volumes, while others appear in volumes dedicated to a particular theme or region. Many will be

---

28. R. Meiggs and D. M. Lewis, *Greek Historical Inscriptions* (rev. ed.; Oxford: Oxford University Press, 1988), no. 1.

29. E.g., L. Threatte, *The Grammar of Attic Inscriptions* (2 vols.; Berlin: de Gruyter, 1980-96). See G. H. R. Horsley, "Epigraphical Grammars," in *New Documents Illustrating Early Christianity. Volume 4: A Review of the Greek Inscriptions and Papyri Published in 1979* (North Ryde, Australia: Ancient History Documentary Research Centre, Macquarie University, 1987), 273.

30. For the latter see M. F. Smith, *The Philosophical Inscription of Diogenes of Oinoanda* (Vienna: Verlag der Österreichischen Akademie der Wissenschaften, 1996).

31. F. Millar, "Epigraphy," in *Sources for Ancient History* (ed. M. Crawford, E. Gabba, F. Millar, and A. M. Snodgrass; Cambridge: Cambridge University Press, 1983), 80–136 (80).

republished in new editions when a study of a particular theme requires a new corpus of inscriptions to be gathered relevant to the topic.

As the focus of this book is on the contribution of inscriptions, some definition of inscriptions is worthwhile. While this would appear to be a straightforward matter—objects carved on stone rather than written on papyrus—the delineation of the corpus has important consequences for the interpretation of the documents themselves. Documentary papyri are of a non-literary nature and include such topics as wills, receipts, letters, court proceedings, and contracts. Therefore, they have proven indispensable for reconstructing the language of personal communication, often without the (Atticist) refinement imposed on literary language. The Duke Data Bank has digitized the papyri, but it does not contain exclusively those documents written on the material papyrus (and parchment). Rather the content of the texts determined their inclusion, such that the Databank contains some non-official inscriptions in the form of ostraca and wooden tablets. Documents digitized in the separate database for inscriptions (Packhum) are those considered official or semi-official, although also included are some graffiti. Distinguishing between sources based on type of material is functionally irrelevant when consulting the databases and is largely artificial. There is a presupposition that the Packhum inscriptions will contain more formal language, and therefore be less suited for comparison with biblical Greek. However, documentary papyri and inscriptions are varied in genre and style, a variation made all the more acute by the differing educational levels of the scribes.[32] The focus on inscriptions in this study is practical, in order to examine a dataset that has been neglected so far. This separation, nevertheless, between documents by content also accounts for the focus in linguistic research so far on papyri over inscriptions.

Inscriptions have been a source available to the scholar far longer than the majority of papyri. They began to be systematically recorded from the seventeenth century onwards. Although occasional studies on the Bible did utilize such epigraphic evidence,[33] they were in the minority. As Horsley has observed,[34] it took some time for the importance of inscriptions

---

32. See R. S. Bagnall, *Everyday Writing in the Graeco-Roman East* (Sather Classical Lectures 69; Berkeley, CA: University of California Press, 2011), 3.

33. Notable in this regard is Walch, *Observationes in Matthaeum.*

34. G. H. R. Horsley, "Epigraphy as an Ancilla to the Study of the Greek Bible: A Propos of a Recent Anthology of Inscriptions," *Bib* 79 (1998): 258–67 (258). It should be noted that the article by D. Lincicum, "The Epigraphic Habit and the Biblical Text: Inscriptions as a Source for the Study of the Greek Bible," *BIOSCS* 41 (2008): 84–92, despite the title, deals with the different topic of biblical quotations within Jewish or Christian inscriptions, and not the evidence from Greek inscriptions taken more broadly.

for biblical research to be appreciated, and even then it might not have been the case were it not, ironically, for the discovery of large numbers of papyri in Egypt, which drew attention to the importance of documentary evidence.

This neglect is despite the long interest that has been shown in inscriptions for historical research by ancient historians.[35] Those scholars who were aware of the lexicographic importance of the inscriptions were often caught up in the papyrological evidence and were delayed for various reasons from venturing upon the inscriptions. It has been shown that Deissmann, who occasionally drew on inscriptions but paid greater attention to papyri, had hoped to devote more time to the epigraphic evidence, until he was diverted by the outbreak of the First World War.[36] As Horsley has shown, Deissmann seems to advise Moulton not to draw too heavily on inscriptions and only use the indices of recently published volumes.[37] Accordingly, Moulton and Milligan even seem to have avoided inscriptions, leaving them for Deissmann to include in his planned, but never completed, new lexicon.[38] Personal circumstances then resulted in the abandonment of inscriptions amid the first flush of excitement over documentary sources.

The recognition of the importance of inscriptions was seen in the course of the twentieth century, although primarily for historical reconstruction of the New Testament world.[39] Gabba's compendium was the first major contribution, presenting 35 inscriptions throwing light on the Bible, especially the New Testament.[40] His work, republished more recently by Boffo with eleven new inscriptions (one deletion) and more extensive commentary,[41] touches only occasionally on lexicography,[42]

35. On which, see W. Stenhouse, *Reading Inscriptions and Writing Ancient History: Historical Scholarship in the Late Renaissance* (BICSSup 86; London: Institute of Classical Studies, 2005).

36. This is apparent from his correspondence with J. H. Moulton, as analysed by G. H. R. Horsley, "The Origin and Scope of Moulton and Milligan's *Vocabulary of the Greek Testament*, and Deissmann's Planned New Testament Lexicon. Some Unpublished Letters of G. A. Deissmann to J. H. Moulton," *BJRL* 76 (1994): 187–216.

37. Horsley, "The Origin and Scope," 96. Cf. Horsley, "Epigraphy as an Ancilla," 259.

38. Horsley: "The Origin and Scope," 213.

39. Even this, though, is considered a slow process. See R. Oster, "The Ephesian Artemis 'Whom All Asia and the World Worship' (Acts 19:27): Representative Epigraphical Testimony to Ἄρτεμις Ἐφεσία outside Ephesos," in *Transmission and Reception: New Testament Text-critical and Exegetical Studies* (ed. D. C. Parker; Texts and Studies. Third series 4; Piscataway, NJ: Gorgias, 2006), 212–31 (213).

40. E. Gabba, *Iscrizioni greche e latine per lo studio della Bibbia* (Sintesi dell'oriente e della Bibbia 3; Rome: Marietti, 1958).

41. L. Boffo, *Iscrizioni greche e latine per lo studio della Bibbia* (Biblioteca di storia e storiografia dei tempi biblici 9; Brescia: Paideia, 1994). This work is the object of Horsley's review, "Epigraphy as an Ancilla."

42. A rare example is εὐεργέτης in Luke 22:25.

considering historical and theological questions that are illuminated by ancient inscriptions. In New Testament lexicography, the Bauer tradition stands preeminent. It holds a special place in its incorporation of documentary sources, although since its earlier manifestations it has only made occasional additions. The reliance on secondary tools, such as Moulton and Milligan in the earlier editions[43] and *New Documents* in the latest,[44] indicate the lack of a systematic investigation of new data.

3. Inscriptions and Greek lexicons

An important recent resource is the material published in the series *New Documents Illustrating Early Christianity*, which presents equally inscriptions and papyri. Since it focuses on the New Testament, the light it throws on the Septuagint is limited, but helpful. The omission of inscriptions from biblical lexicography is indicative of a broader neglect in Greek lexicography, where occasional if brief studies have appeared. Searles's dissertation early on indicated the importance of inscriptions in general for lexicographic work, and especially how they attest to many new or rare words.[45] The majority of her book catalogues new words found in inscriptions, as well as rare words and meanings. A small section on poetical words in prose inscriptions highlights a problem in determining the register of words, an issue to which we will return in chapter 5. Ferguson's study of legal terms common to Macedonian inscriptions and the New Testament comprises samples with discussion,[46] but reviewers were not favorable to the small light it shed.

Among lexicons the revision by Wilhelm Crönert of Passow's *Wörterbuch der griechischen Sprache* (1913) had the ambitious goal[47] of conscientiously incorporating papyri and inscriptions, the former up to the Byzantine period.[48] It was also to contain a whole range of data, including the scholiasts, the Septuagint and the New Testament. Its ambition was probably the cause of its downfall, as it did not last more than one year,

---

43. J. A. L. Lee, *A History of New Testament Lexicography* (New York: Peter Lang, 2003),144.

44. Explicitly stated in the preface: BDAG, ix.

45. H. M. Searles, *A Lexicographical Study of the Greek Inscriptions* (Studies in Classical Philology 2; Chicago, IL: University of Chicago Press, 1899).

46. W. D. Ferguson, *The Legal Terms Common to the Macedonian Greek Inscriptions and the New Testament* (Chicago, IL: University of Chicago Press, 1913).

47. See the comments of the reviewer C. Knapp, in *The Classical Weekly* 7.16 (1914): 121.

48. F. Passow, *Wörterbuch der griechischen Sprache, Völlig neu bearb. Wilhelm Crönert* (Göttingen: Vandenhoeck and Ruprecht, 1913).

during which three folios saw the light of day. Likewise, F. Preisigke drew on epigraphic material from a range of sources (including inscriptions, ostraca, and coins), as did its revisions by E. Kiessling, and supplements, but as the title implies, the focus was on papyri first.[49] LSJ, itself dependent on Passow, remains the most reliable source for the lexicographic import of inscriptions, but even then it is considerably deficient in comparison to papyri, and the inconsistent use of inscriptions in the *Supplement* only compounded the problem.[50] Since the revision by Jones and MacKenzie, inscriptions were consistently cited in LSJ, even if inevitably older editions of the inscriptions were used. The *Supplements* to LSJ have, nevertheless, proven useful in their addition of new inscriptional material providing further examples of words hitherto only known in biblical and related literature.[51] As already noted, though, material was incorporated in a haphazard fashion, dependent to an extent upon informants and corrections from readers.[52]

The new *Diccionario Griego-Español* (DGE) aims to rectify this situation by incorporating far more documentary evidence than ever before. The progress of the *Diccionario* has been slow, reaching only the letter *epsilon* after 30 years, and it has not yet had an influence on biblical scholarship.[53] As noted by its editors, the *Diccionario* incorporates far more papyrological and inscriptional material than LSJ. As a result, through its incorporation of new data it is estimated that it will be as much as thirty to fifty percent larger than LSJ.[54] This increase reflects the wealth of material available from inscriptions and other documentary sources. Rodríguez

49. F. Preisigke, *Wörterbuch der griechischen Papyrusurkunden mit Einschluss der griechischen Inschriften, Ausschriften, Ostraka, Mumienschilder usw. aus Ägypten* (3 vols.; Berlin: Selbstverlag der Erben, 1924–).

50. See F. R. Adrados, "Léxico de inscripciones y dialectal," in F. R. Adrados, E. Gangutia, J. López Facal, and C. Serrano Aybar, *Introducción a la lexicografía griega* (Madrid: CSIC, 1977), 169–83 (173–74). An improvement was made in the revised Supplement (ed. P. G. W. Glare and A. A. Thompson; Oxford: Clarendon, 1996), but even then the documentary evidence is cited inconsistently. Adrados ("Ordenadores y lexicografía griega. El Banco de Datos," in Adrados et al., *Introducción*, 212–13) protests that many of the computerized indices now being produced are of authors who are already adequately covered.

51. Lee, *Lexical Study of the Septuagint*, 45, had already noted this, giving examples from the first Supplement of ἀτεκνόω, περιχαλκόω, and σανιδωτός.

52. On the problem of restructuring entries with the addition of new data, see Lee, *History of New Testament Lexicography*, 170.

53. *Diccionario Griego-Español*, redactado bajo la dirección de F. R. Adrados, por E. Gangutia, L. Facal, C. S. Aybar, P. Bádenas y otros colaboradores (Madrid: Instituto Antonio de Nebrija, 1980–). Volume VII was published in 2009, taking the alphabet as far as ἔξαυος.

54. J. L. Facal, "Historia de la lexicografía griega moderna," in F. R. Adrados, E. Gangutia, J. López Facal y C. Serrano Aybar, *Introducción a la lexicografía griega* (Madrid: CSIC, 1977), 107–42 (138–39).

Somolinos indicates the importance of inscriptions alone through a cal-culation of words in the *Diccionario* that are extant only in inscriptions. She determines that in volume V of the DGE (Madrid 1997, ranging from δαίνυμι to διώνυχος) some 250 words of the approximately 7,040 in the volume are documented only in inscriptions, and more than half of these, 173, are *hapax legomena*.[55] In Volume IV (Madrid 1994, covering βασιλευτός to δαίμων), the proportion was similar with 215 words exclu-sively in epigraphic documents, and 136 of these were *hapax legomena*.

The volumes of the *Diccionario* seem to include far more post-classical literary references, which are essential data for the study of biblical Greek and have been incorporated in BDAG but not in Septuagint lexicons. The result is that it should add to the importance of the *Diccionario* for bibli-cal studies. The General Editor, Francisco Adrados, has himself pointed out the immense problem of the disorganized state of Greek epigraphy, also recognizing that the best lexicon has so far been LSJ itself.[56] The situation in papyrology is better, but only by comparison. A project of this sort requires expertise in Archaic, Classical, and Koine Greek, an ability to handle literature from archaic through to late antique times, as well as technical knowledge of documentary sources, be they preserved in in-scriptions or papyri. One must keep abreast of developments in the field, including corrections to readings in new editions of inscriptions and new interpretations.[57]

4. The language of inscriptions

There have been two consequences of an almost exclusive focus on papyri. First, the language of the Septuagint, indeed of biblical Greek, has been given geographic specification through being viewed as the Greek of Egypt. There is a certain tautology here, since the papyri are almost entirely from Egypt, except in the rare cases of chance survival elsewhere: the Herculaneum papyri preserved in the ash of Mt. Vesuvius, the Der-veni papyrus found in a Macedonian necropolis, and the Greek documents uncovered from the Judean desert and other arid regions of the Middle East.[58] Egyptian provenance avoids the question whether any of the books

55. H. Rodríguez Somolinos, "El DGE y la epigrafía griega: el problema de las palabras fantasma (ejemplificación y tipología)," in *La lexicografía griega y el Diccionario Griego-Espa-ñol, DGE. Anejo VI* (ed. F. R. Adrados and J. Rodríguez Somolinos; Madrid: CSIC, 2005), 165–75 (165).

56. Adrados, "Léxico de inscripciones y dialectal," 174.

57. Rodríguez Somolinos, "El DGE y la epigrafía griega."

58. A. Maiuri, *Herculaneum and the Villa of the Papyri* (Novara: Instituto Geografico de Agostini, 1963); D. Sider, *The Library of the Villa dei Papiri at Herculaneum* (Los An-

could be translated elsewhere, or indeed whether one can draw a dialectal or phonological distinction between Greek from Egypt and Greek from elsewhere. Even an apparently Egyptian feature, influenced perhaps by the spoken Egyptian language (as early editors often assumed),[59] could reflect the language more broadly used in the Ptolemaic empire.

The geographical bias of papyri can be counterbalanced by consideration of the inscriptions.[60] It remains true that the papyri may still be important as offering the most likely linguistic match to the Septuagint,[61] but the differentiation that inscriptions offer—the wide diversity of locations and formality of registers—can be seen as an advantage rather than a disadvantage. Inscriptions have been lauded for the richness and diversity of the evidence they provide, offering examples of all lexical fields and registers of the language.[62] As such they could throw a fresh perspective on Septuagint language.

Second, since the papyri from Egypt are mostly documentary, representing private wills, personal letters, and contracts, there has been a tendency to associate the "language of papyri" with "popular" Greek or non-literary Greek.[63] This is to confuse linguistic features with genre and register. Within one genre, such as a letter, one can find different registers and types of linguistic features, dependent upon the author and the intended recipient. What the papyri show is that biblical Greek is for the most part contemporary Greek, in vocabulary, morphology, and syntax,

---

geles: J. Paul Getty Museum, 2005); A. Laks and G. W. Most, eds., *Studies on the Derveni Papyrus* (Oxford: Oxford University Press, 1997); H. M. Cotton and A. Yardeni, *Discoveries in the Judaean Desert: Volume XXVII. Aramaic, Hebrew and Greek Documentary Texts from Naḥal Ḥever and Other Sites* (Oxford: Clarendon, 1997).

59. The tendency of some editors to attribute peculiarities in Greek papyri to Egyptian interference has begun to be questioned. See, e.g., T. V. Evans, "Standard *Koine* Greek in Third Century BC Papyri," in *Proceedings of the Twenty-Fifth International Congress of Papyrology, Ann Arbor 2007* (ed. T. Gagos; Ann Arbor, MI: University of Michigan Press, 2010), 211–20; and T. V. Evans, "Complaints of the Natives in a Greek Dress: the Zenon Archive and the Problem of Egyptian Interference," in *Multilingualism in the Graeco-Roman Worlds* (ed. A. Mullen and P. James; Cambridge: Cambridge University Press, 2012), 106–23.

60. F. Millar, "Epigraphy," in *Sources for Ancient History* (ed. M. Crawford, E. Gabba, F. Millar, and A. M. Snodgrass; Cambridge: Cambridge University Press, 1983), 80–136 (80–81).

61. So T. V. Evans, "The Use of Linguistic Criteria for Dating Septuagint Books," *BIOSCS* 43 (2010): 5–22 (12).

62. So Rodríguez Somolinos, "El DGE y la epigrafía griega," 165.

63. This is a tendency in the helpful summary of research on the language in N. Fernández Marcos, *The Septuagint in Context: Introduction to the Greek Versions of the Bible* (Leiden: Brill, 2000), 14. He does though, at the same place, recognize the diversity in Koine, an important point that the inscriptions can contribute to. See too J. Joosten, "Le milieu producteur du Pentateuque grec," *REJ* 165 (2006): 349–61 (352).

but to determine whether it is formal or popular, literary or sub-literary, is a separate question of analysis of the documents. As has already been shown, the genres of papyri vary considerably and the styles of writers differ noticeably,[64] even authors of documentary texts aiming at some literary pretension.[65] The literary level is dependent on the linguistic proficiency and intention of the author rather than on the writing material. Nonetheless, even Deissmann, who had a grasp of both inscriptions and papyri, favored the papyri for this very reason:

> That this quality [proximity to biblical Greek] inheres especially in the papyri is not a matter of accident, since they more nearly concern private and common life. The inscriptions, which are public, are often, particularly when official, consciously made to approach the norms of literary style; while the papyri are often unpolished and express the many needs and varying situations of the daily life of the mass of the population. And this general situation is borne out by the formulas and usage of legal procedure.[66]

In this assessment Deissmann has been criticized for going too far, although a legacy of such ideas can still be traced in writings. Deissmann was caught up in the debates of his age and sought to see in the language of the Bible the constitutive character of the early church.[67] The terms we use, however, such as "standard," "non-standard," "vulgar," or "popular," are often so vague that it is unclear precisely what they are noting as distinctive without further clarification and refinement.[68]

---

64. J. A. L. Lee, "Some Features of the Speech of Jesus in Mark's Gospel," *NovT* 27 (1985): 1–26 (9); G. H. R. Horsley, "Koine or Atticism—A Misleading Dichotomy," in *New Documents Illustrating Early Christianity, 5: Linguistic Essays* (North Ryde, Australia: Ancient History Documentary Research Centre, Macquarie University, 1989), 41–48 (44–45).

65. See, e.g., T. Morgan, *Literate Education in the Hellenistic and Roman Worlds* (Cambridge Classical Studies; Cambridge: Cambridge University Press, 1998), 219–26. The existence of varying degrees of literary features in documentary texts is also noted by Evans, "Standard *Koine*." See too J. K. Aitken, "The Language of the Septuagint and Jewish Greek Identity," in *The Jewish-Greek Tradition in Antiquity and the Byzantine Empire* (ed. J. K. Aitken and J. Carleton Paget; Cambridge: Cambridge University Press, 2014), forthcoming.

66. "Hellenistic Greek," 213.

67. H. T. Gamble, *Books and Readers in the Early Church: A History of Early Christian Texts* (New Haven: Yale University Press, 1995), 13–14. See too A. L. A. Hogeterp, "New Testament Greek as Popular Speech: Adolf Deissmann in Retrospect: A Case Study in Luke's Greek," *ZNW* 102 (2011): 178–200.

68. Some programmatic statements on this point are made by T. V. Evans and D. D. Obbink, "Introduction," in *The Language of the Papyri* (ed. T. V. Evans and D. D. Obbink; Oxford: Oxford University Press, 2009), 1–12 (9–11).

Inscriptions witness to a variety of registers of Greek,[69] from monumental inscriptions of a literary nature that often present the king or governor in fine literary terms to more colloquial expressions, found for example in graffiti.[70] The social context is varied too, ranging from political and legal decrees to religious texts, sacred laws, hymns, private communications, and financial notes. Some of the examples examined in this volume are from religious hymns and dedications carved on walls or on monuments, which cannot easily be classified by social register. While the words in such cases are not standard in literature, they do seem to be distinctive to such religious contexts. They do not appear, therefore, to be merely everyday language, but specific language of religious praise that is neither vernacular nor high literary.

While classical standards remained important in the educational system of the Graeco-Roman world, new words were created or came to be acceptable in later literature that would not appear earlier. A number of terms that could be classed as vulgar or non-classical begin to appear in literature by the Roman period. Thus, ῥύμη to denote a street, as in Sir 9:7, is disapproved of by Atticist purists (Phrynichus, *Eclogues* 383), but then appears in Chariton's *Callirhoe* (1.1.13, first or second century C.E.) and in the more literary of Jewish compositions, *The Sibylline Oracles* (3.364). Although not used in classical Greek literature for "street," it had become so common in the vernacular that it could be used in Chariton, who was not unaffected by the Atticist movement.[71] At the same time the reverse can happen, such as when an originally poetic word is absorbed into prose usage, as the inscriptions testify.[72]

5. *The omission of inscriptions*

No one type of evidence should take priority in lexicographic work. Inevitably we prefer the more familiar, such as literature, over the less familiar or difficult to handle, such as inscriptions. We also favor those

69. Noted by J. H. Moulton, "The Science of Language and the Study of the NT," in *The Christian Religion in the Study and in the Street* (London: Hodder and Stoughton, 1919), 117–44 (134). See Horsley, "Origin and Scope."

70. The issue of register, especially in Koine, is an understudied area, but of obvious significance for examining biblical Greek. Among studies we should note S. E. Porter, ed., *Diglossia and Other Topics in New Testament Linguistics* (Sheffield: Sheffield Academic Press, 2000), and some of the essays in A. Georgakopoulou and M. S. Silk, eds., *Standard Languages and Language Standards: Greek, Past and Present* (Farnham: Ashgate, 2009).

71. C. Hernández Lara, "Rhetorical Aspects of Chariton of Aphrodisias," *Giornale Italiano di Filologia* 42 (1990): 267–74.

72. See Searles, *Lexicographical Study*, 109–14.

sources that have received greater attention in scholarship, such as papyri, whose importance has been brought into prominence. But this is not an excuse to minimize any one record. An attestation of a word is of equal value whatever the source, taking into account date, genre, and reliability of the reading. Evidence that is unfamiliar can be overlooked in large comprehensive works such as the *Theological Dictionary of the New Testament*. The example of ἅγιος was noted some time ago by Barr as a word which the reference works misrepresent regarding its attestations.[73] It was presumed to be rare in non-biblical Greek, implying that the biblical writers had chosen it as an alternative to the more popular ἱερός. Such rare words were seen to be less affected by the taint of Hellenistic religion.[74] In short, Barr showed how ἅγιος is well attested in Classical and Hellenistic times, and how scholars would cite inscriptional evidence that showed the word was not unique to the Septuagint, but would discount those citations without reason.[75]

More recent publications are not immune from the problem. De Crom, for example, successfully demonstrates how the papyri illustrate the lexicon of the Greek Song of Songs.[76] He notes that this is not merely of lexicographic interest, but can also be used to account for translation choices and to clarify text-critical problems. Importantly, he shows that the parallels with papyri do not prove that a word is exclusively Egyptian in provenance.[77] The one limitation to De Crom's analysis is that he focuses solely on papyri, despite his recognition that the attention given to the numerous *Egyptian* papyri can lead to a false perspective.[78] Given the detail in his research, his omission of inscriptions does not affect his overall conclusions. However, it does mean that he must speculate unnecessarily when evidence is indeed available from the epigraphic sources. Therefore, since he finds no attestation of the verb ἐκλοχίζω (Cant 5:10) outside the

---

73. J. Barr, *The Semantics of Biblical Language* (London: Oxford University Press, 1961), 282–86, esp. 283–84.

74. See O. Procksch, "ἅγιος, etc.," in *Theologisches Wörterbuch zum Neuen Testament* (ed. G. Kittel and G. Friedrich; 11 vols.; Stuttgart: Kohlhammer, 1932–79), 1: 87–116.

75. So Procksch, "ἅγιος, etc.," citing the Ptolemaic inscription *Ditt. Or.* (= OGIS) 56.59, which he had taken from M. Flashar, "Exegetische Studien zum Septuagintapsalter," *ZAW* 32 (1912): 81–116, 161–89, 241–68 (245).

76. D. De Crom, "The Lexicon of LXX Canticles and Greco-Roman Papyri," *ZAW* 124 (2012): 255–62.

77. De Crom, "Lexicon of LXX Canticles," 256–57, 262.

78. "If parallels with papyri from Ptolemaic and Roman Egypt appear more numerous, it should always be kept in mind that the evidence is naturally slanted towards Egypt, both through the wealth of materials preserved in the Egyptian climate and through the huge amount of scholarly attention they have received in the past century" (De Crom, "Lexicon of LXX Canticles," 262).

Septuagint, he explains it on the basis of etymology and by analogy with καταλογίζω.[79] There is, though, one occurrence of this word, but it is in an inscription (SB 1:4206.239) rather than in a papyrus. As will be explained (chapter 4), that one occurrence in an inscription comes from the same time period as Septuagint Song of Songs and exhibits a remarkably similar usage.[80] At other times his data could have been bolstered by recourse to inscriptions, especially when he was being open regarding the provenance of the translation.

A further problem appears to be the blindness to inscriptional evidence among some scholars. Under the entry for ὁρμίσκος in LEH (446) the abbreviation for a neologism is given, which in LEH signifies "that the word in question was probably not used before the time of composition of the LXX."[81] Consultation of LSJ (1253) should have thrown this assumption into question, since in the relevant entry there are two references given preceding the Septuagint (in this case Cant 1:10), indicating that they are earlier in date:

> ὁρμίσκος, ὁ, Dim. of ὅρμος, *small necklace*, IGl².317.6, Chares 3 J., LXX *Ca.*1.10, *IG*l²(8).51.18 (Imbros, ii B. C.), Ph.1.665, Ael. *NA*8.4.[82]

One can be forgiven for excluding the *Sentences of Menander* by Chares, since the late fourth-century gnomic poet's work is preserved in fragments and therefore could be susceptible to corruption. In this case, though, the *Sentences* are found in a papyrus (TM 65709; LDAB 6963) originally dated to the third century B.C.E. (Mertens-Pack) and therefore even the actual evidence could be from the time of the early Septuagint books.[83] However, this date remains disputed and some would date it much later (second century C.E.). The inscriptional evidence recorded in LSJ is less problematic (IG I 2.317.6 = IG I 3.390).[84] As would be implied by the Attic inscription being listed in LSJ before the Septuagint, it is indeed dated to the late fifth century (420–405 B.C.E.), as are a number of very similar inscriptions with this word included, though some are badly damaged

---

79. De Crom, "Lexicon of LXX Canticles," 258–59.

80. This corroborating evidence has already been noted in J. K. Aitken, "Context of Situation in Biblical Lexica," in *Foundations for Syriac Lexicography III: Colloquia of the International Syriac Language Project* (ed. J. Dyk and W. van Peursen; Perspectives on Syriac Linguistics 4; Piscataway, NJ: Gorgias, 2008), 181–201 (195–96).

81. LEH xiv.

82. LSJ 1253.

83. G. A. Gerhard, *Charētos gnōmai* (Heidelberg: C. Winter, 1912), 13.

84. F. Hiller von Gaertringen, *Inscriptiones Graecae. Inscriptiones Atticae Euclidis anno anteriores, editio minor* (Berlin: de Gruyter, 1924).

(e.g., IG I 3.356.52; 359.4) and some fully reconstructed by editors (e.g., IG I 3.355.26; 357.52).[85] It would seem that the inscriptional evidence has simply been passed over. The citation of ὁρμίσκος as a neologism in LEH then led De Crom to devote some space to showing that it was not a coinage of the Septuagint, even though this should never have been in question in the first place. He was successful nonetheless in demonstrating that the word could not be a Septuagint neologism when it is found in a third-century B.C.E. papyrus (P.Mich. 3.173 [TM 8337]), though it might now be dated later. De Crom even mentions that there is epigraphic evidence cited in LSJ, but does not examine it any further or consider that it might obviate further discussion.

Similar problems appear in New Testament studies. Mardaga identifies five previously unattested words in John's Gospel, but by relying on the existing tools she does not identify one of them in an earlier inscription.[86] For the term νιπτήρ 'basin' (John 13:5) she recognizes that it occurs in a Roman-era inscription from Cyprus (GDI 123.8),[87] information that she gleans from BDAG (674), which has itself not been updated.[88] The noun νιπτήρ 'basin' is a natural derivation from the verb νίπτω (νίζω) 'to wash' and therefore it would be no surprise to find it earlier. Indeed, its seventeen appearances in the New Testament, as noted by Mardaga, should already have alerted her to the likelihood of it not being a coinage of the biblical authors. In addition we might note the use of the compound ποδανιπτήρ 'basin for washing feet' attested as early as Herodotus (2.272) and frequent in Attic inscriptions (LSJ 1426). A systematic consultation of the epigraphic evidence reveals that νιπτήρ could indeed be used earlier, as it is found in an inventory list from a temple in Delos (IDelos 372.29; 200 B.C.E.).

These observations are not to criticize the scholars concerned specifically, because they have made important lexicological observations nonetheless. De Crom in particular has advanced more than most in gleaning insights from documentary sources. Rather, the scholars are inheritors of a tradition that simply overlooks inscriptional data for lexicography. It may be in part due to the ease with which one might literally overlook such brief abbreviations in LSJ as *IGI*². It is also reflective of a more general

---

85. It is admitted in LEH (xiv) that inscriptions are notoriously difficult to date, but in this case there seems no reason to question the date or exclude the evidence.

86. H. Mardaga, "Hapax Legomena and the Idiolect of John," *NovT* 56 (2014): 134–53.

87. Mardaga, "Hapax Legomena," 152.

88. Mardaga, "Hapax Legomena," 152; cf. n. 78. She also cites the same sources as BDAG, without updating either.

tendency to prioritize literature and papyri over other evidence. Today most scholars recognize the importance of papyri and accept the insights of Deissmann and his successors, even if they are few in number who incorporate papyri into Septuagint lexicography. In contrast, inscriptions have been overshadowed by the success of the case for papyri.

CHAPTER 3

Working with Greek Inscriptions

Inscriptions present particular difficulties for the lexicographer, especially for those in biblical studies who are without experience in using them. Moulton himself recognized the challenges posed by inscriptions and admitted it would have been a hopeless task to include them systematically in his *Vocabulary*.[1] Even today it can be a daunting prospect for those wishing to embark on epigraphic research. Simply identifying and locating the texts, as well as understanding the conventions used can be difficult. The electronic revolution has made the task far more manageable, but many of the principal hurdles remain the same. A greater number of accessible resources are becoming available, although from the start papyrologists have been more organized than epigraphists in developing tools and electronic databases.[2] Epigraphic volumes rarely offer translations of the inscriptions, and in older works the notes are usually found in Latin. Too few volumes indicate any date for an inscription (particularly in the case of the IG volumes) and hence this often must be determined by each reader.[3] In contrast to the tools for papyri, there is no agreed reference system for inscriptions, complicating the identification of a text.[4] Electronic edi-

---

1. J. H. Moulton and G. Milligan, *The Vocabulary of the Greek Testament Illustrated from the Papyri and Other Non-Literary Sources* (8 fascicles; London: Hodder and Stoughton, 1914–29), 1: v (this is published in the first volume, but not included in the one-volume complete edition, published in 1930). See also G. H. R. Horsley, "The Greek Documentary Evidence and NT Lexical Study: Some Soundings," in *New Documents Illustrating Early Christianity. Volume 5: Linguistic Essays* (North Ryde, Australia: Ancient History Documentary Research Centre, Macquarie University, 1989), 67–94.

2. The contrast is noted by G. H. R. Horsley, "Epigraphy as an Ancilla to the Study of the Greek Bible: A Propos of a Recent Anthology of Inscriptions," *Bib* 79 (1998): 258–67 (259).

3. There has been circulating privately the proposed datings by D. F. McCabe, which were embedded in the PHI-7 CD-Rom prepared by the Packard Humanities Institute. Much of the search software that was originally available for the CD-Rom was not designed to display these dates. Since these inscriptions have become available on the web the dates have been displayed, where known (Online: epigraphy.packhum.org).

4. A proposal for a systematisation of references has been put forward by G. H. R. Horsley and J. A. L. Lee, "A Preliminary Checklist of Abbreviations of Greek Epigraphic

tions have been produced for searching and analyzing inscriptions, such as the Packard Humanities Institute (PHI/Packhum) "Searchable Greek Inscriptions"[5] or individual Epidoc projects like the Aphrodisias Inscriptions.[6] While the Epidoc projects only cover small corpora, the Packhum inscriptions database is not as advanced or up-to-date as the Duke Data Bank of Documentary papyri.

The intention in this chapter is to provide a guide through some of the practicalities of working with inscriptions. While some issues are shared with papyri, some are distinct to the inscriptions. There are a number of conventions and practices that are familiar to those working in the field, and knowledge of these is often assumed in the databases and published editions without any guidance offered. To those new to the area or those in biblical studies who will not be familiar with the issues or resources, it will be helpful to describe them. In this way it is hoped that others can tread a similar path. The Appendix to this book lists in a convenient fashion the tools discussed here along with other resources.

1. *"First catch your hare": Gathering the lexical data*

The first task is of course to "catch your hare"—find the words in inscriptions. There are no word lists, however, for inscriptions, necessitating a range of methods for searching. The fastest and easiest way is to begin with an electronic search. And yet the tools available, while impressive in their content, offer very little in the way of user instructions or guidance.

a. *The origins of the data*

Most readers will be familiar with the Thesaurus Linguae Graecae (TLG), which allows the searching of Greek literature from Homer to 1453 C.E. (the fall of Byzantium). It was originally available on CD-Rom, but now can be accessed online by those with a subscription.[7] The equivalent for inscriptions and papyri used to be the CD-Rom PHI-7, purchased from the Packard Humanities Institute. The material from this CD-Rom can now be accessed online, without any subscription, divided between two websites, one for inscriptions and one for papyri. Online publication allows for regular updates and corrections, although what additions have been made since the CD-Rom are not listed. The papyri in the Duke Data

---

Volumes," *Epigraphica* 56 (1994): 129–69. Abbreviations here follow their preliminary checklist.

   5. Online: epigraphy.packhum.org/inscriptions/.

   6. Online: www.epapp.kcl.ac.uk/.

   7. Online: www.tlg.uci.edu/.

Bank of Documentary Papyri are found online on the papyri.info website, although the data can never be as up-to-date as newly published volumes of papyri. Therefore indices of published volumes should still be consulted, especially recently published editions. Nonetheless an important service has been provided by the "Heidelberger WörterListen," a project of the Instituts für Papyrologie at the University of Heidelberg.[8] This is a regularly updated consolidated list of words extracted from new publications of papyri, providing a reference to the relevant published volumes.

There is no equivalent to the "WörterListen" for inscriptions. The PHI CD-Rom only contained epigraphic data up to 1995, and even then this was not comprehensive. For example, many inscriptions were entered according to region rather than by year, and although Greek inscriptions from the *Supplementum Epigraphicum Graecum* (SEG) volumes were entered, many inscriptions from Italy up to 1995 were not. Since the data has been made available online at epigraphy.packhum.org, the list of inscriptions added from 2007 onwards can be found by clicking on "Last Update" on the homepage. It does not, however, provide a complete list of contents. Hence, once more it is advisable whenever a search is undertaken to consult recently published volumes of inscriptions and the volumes of SEG.[9] Consolidated indexes have been published for the SEG for the years 1976–95; the indexes record all the words mentioned in the publications of those volumes. From after that date the individual indexes of each volume can be consulted. The latest edition of SEG (volume LX) takes us up to the year 2010.[10] For those with library subscriptions, the SEG is now online allowing one to search for words with ease. All available evidence must be used in any work at an advanced level, especially where we have an advantage over our predecessors by having tools that were simply not available when our lexicons were made.[11]

b. Searching the databases

Unlike TLG, which uses an automatic lemmatizer, or commercial biblical search programs, which have been manually lemmatized, the texts

---

8. Online: www.zaw.uni-heidelberg.de/hps/pap/WL/WL.pdf. The full name is "WörterListen aus den Registern von Publikationen griechischer und lateinischer dokumentarischer Papyri und Ostraka," compiled under the direction of D. Hagedorn.

9. Despite the limitations to Preisigke's *Wörterbuch*, it is still far superior to anything available for inscriptions.

10. *Supplementum Epigraphicum Graecum, LX (2010)* (ed. A. Chaniotis, T. Corsten, and R. A. Tybout; Leiden: Brill, 2013).

11. J. A. L. Lee, "The Present State of Lexicography of Ancient Greek," in *Biblical Greek Language and Lexicography: Essays in Honor of Frederick W. Danker* (ed. B. Taylor, J. A. L. Lee, P. Burton, and R. Whitaker; Grand Rapids, MI: Eerdmans, 2004), 66–74 (67).

in the Duke Data Bank of Papyri and the Packhum Epigraphy database are not lemmatized. Searching therefore requires consideration of all the possible forms, the various conjugations and declensions, even if it can lead to wading through some irrelevant forms. One should bear in mind typical phonetic spelling variants, although these are usually normalized in the apparatus of the databases or using appropriate sigla in the texts and therefore do appear in the searches. As there are no lexicons available for such material, the researcher might well have to translate the texts and then must make his or her own judgment to determine whether or not it is the lexical form desired.

The Packhum site includes a guide ("Help") to the search functions one can use. Most useful is the hash character (#) to mark a word break, but one can also use such Boolean operators as 'or' (^), 'and' (&), and 'near' (~). The greatest difficulty is ensuring coverage of all the morphological forms of a word. A search using καταλαμ, for example, will find many forms of καταλαμβάνω, but not with the augment (κατε-) or in the strong aorist form (-λαβ-). Accordingly, it is helpful to have a complete list of morphological forms to ensure all are covered in the search options. Consultation of LSJ where many of the forms are given can assist in this. Those with a subscription to TLG can have that database list all the known forms of a word and use this as the basis for their searches.

2. *Identifying volumes*

There is a lack of consistency in publications regarding the citation of inscriptions, and sometimes identifying a particular abbreviation can be difficult. Whereas for papyri and ostraca there is an agreed "Checklist of Greek, Latin, Demotic and Coptic Papyri,"[12] no such universal agreement exists among epigraphists. The inconsistency extends beyond the abbreviations, but can include volume numbers, years, reference numbers of inscriptions, or even pages. Horsley and Lee have drawn up a preliminary "checklist" for inscriptions,[13] and, given their inclusion of alternative reference systems, it can also be helpful for identifying less familiar abbreviations. The CLAROS database, under the auspices of the *Diccionario Griego-Español* project, is also an important tool.[14] It provides bibliographic references to newer publications of an inscription, allowing the

---

12. Although published in hardcopy, now in its fifth edition, it is most readily available online: library.duke.edu/rubenstein/scriptorium/papyrus/texts/clist.html.

13. Horsley and Lee, "Preliminary Checklist."

14. "CLAROS. Concordance of Greek inscriptions" [Online: www.dge.filol.csic.es/claros/cnc/2cnc.htm].

researcher to discover earlier or later editions of the same inscription. This is essential for checking the references and abbreviations in new editions, and then for ensuring there are no new suggestions for the reading of the letters. Inevitably, when feasible, researchers should examine photographs and make their own judgment on the reading of an inscription.

The Trismegistos database, begun in 2005, has revolutionized work on the Greek papyri.[15] It has assigned a unique number to each papyrus (TM reference), allowing each papyrus to be identified even where it has been republished under different reference systems. It also provides basic information (metadata) on the documents. It has inevitably focused on Egypt, initially Greco-Roman but soon expanding its range to cover all papyrological documents between 800 B.C.E. and 800 C.E. Documents from after 800, largely in Coptic and Arabic, are also now gradually being entered. Trismegistos has begun to include inscriptions too since for the study of Egypt it would be artificial to exclude them from the evidence, and it currently has approximately 85 percent of inscriptions from Egypt. Unfortunately this only covers Egypt and not the vast quantities of inscriptions from elsewhere, but where possible the TM number has been included in this book.

3. Dating inscriptions

It is important to know when the word is attested to appreciate its relevance for the Septuagint. An earlier or contemporaneous use can justifiably be used as comparative data, while a much later one must be used with caution. Indeed, it is possible in the case of a later inscription that the Septuagint or, more accurately, biblical usage has influenced the language. Determining the date of an inscription is not always easy, however, especially where published editions do not mark it. There are a number of issues, therefore, of which the researcher should be aware.

a. Understanding dating conventions

An inscription will at times include an explicit dating formula which is then indicated in published editions. Even without an explicit formula—such as a regnal or consulate year—scholars have often determined the date of an inscription and included it either in the published version or at least in the online Packhum database. This is not the end of the problem, though, as there is considerable inconsistency in the dating system used and little guidance for interpreting it. At times the indicators B.C.E. or C.E. are entirely omitted, leaving only a number, and when the century is indi-

---

15. Online: www.trismegistos.org.

cated it can be given in Latin, German, Italian, or English abbreviation.[16] Even if this is consistent in individual volumes, when those volumes are combined into one database, the results are confusing. Thus, the standard BC and AD are frequent, but so too are the following assorted abbreviations:

a.	*ante Christum* (B.C.E.);
a.C.	*ante Christum / avanti Cristo* (B.C.E.);
ac	after Christ (C.E.!);
aet. Christ.	Christian era (C.E.);
c.	century, when after a date;
c.	*circa*, when before a date;
ca.	*circa*;
Jh.	Jahrhundert (century);
med.	middle (of a century);
n.Chr.	nach Christus (C.E.);
p.	*post Christum* (C.E.);
s.	*saeculum* (century);
sac	*saeculum ante Christum* (B.C.E.);
v.Chr.	vor Christus (B.C.E.).

A superscript [b] denotes the beginning of the century (such as 3^b in IEph 1060 = PHI Ephesos 649), while a superscript [c] denotes the end of the century ($2^c/3$ signifying end of the second or the third century in IEph 1587b = Ephesos 640). A superscript number [2] apparently denotes the second half of a century, as in $2^2/3$ (IEph 2928 = Ephesos 606). Both Roman numerals (I, II, etc.) and Arabic numbers (1st, 2nd, etc.) are used for centuries.

b. Means of determining date

If, as is often the case, a date is not indicated in the edition, some attempt must be made to date the inscription. Fortunately, many Roman inscriptions can often be identified by Roman names transliterated in Greek or by the names of Emperors. Christian inscriptions too, which can be discounted as independent attestation when Septuagint usage is influential, are usually clear from Christian terminology or symbols. Nevertheless, many inscriptions without political authorization or such specific terminology cannot be so easily dated, and the researcher must resort to other means.

---

16. See further J. A. L. Lee, "The Vocabulary of the Septuagint and Documentary Evidence," in *Handbuch zur Septuaginta: IV Sprache* (ed. E. Bons and J. Joosten; Gütersloh: Gütersloher Verlagshaus), forthcoming.

In cases of uncertainty specialist epigraphers are often able to suggest a date within a given period by paleographic means, although this is not always the most reliable method of dating. There are means at our disposal to discover many of the dates, reserving the consultation of the specialist for only the most difficult examples. The online publication of inscriptions by Packhum, made available since my own research began, includes dates not accessible elsewhere, thanks to the incorporation of McCabe's notes. Where a date is not given, it might be found in a republication of an inscription, such as in SEG. Here the CLAROS database is essential for tracing later publications or new editions of any inscription. There are a number of indicators in inscriptions that can also assist in identifying a date, or at least a general period into which the inscription fits. McLean has helpfully summarized many of these interpretative strategies.[17] These include determining events or persons referred to in the texts, identifying titles or official terms particular to periods (such as Roman titles used in provinces), or finding physical associations between the inscription and archaeological sites.

In addition, while one particular inscription may not be dated, others in the same collection or from the same region, and reflecting similar language and themes, might be. From this one can infer a similar date is likely for the inscription under consideration. Alternatively, after identifying the subject matter of an inscription, consultation of studies on that subject can lead to an indication or discussion of dating of the evidence. Such research can be time-consuming and at times reliant on chance, but it is essential for careful use of the inscriptions. For a researcher interested in lexicography or the Septuagint, it can be frustrating to devote such time in unchartered waters, but the gains of interdisciplinary research should outweigh the labors.

c. Adjudicating between multiple dates

A problem arises where there is debate over a date, and the one inscription will have different dates in different editions. This is regularly encountered when the same text is reproduced more than once in a database owing to its appearance in different editions. One example is that of the Praeneste mosaic whose publication as IG XIV 1302 is marked by Packhum as "reign of Hadrian?" However, in the same database it is reproduced from SEG 45:1452 and the date is given as "*ca.* 120–110 BC." Consultation of the text confirms that the inscription is the same in each,

---

17. B. H. McLean, *An Introduction to Greek Epigraphy of the Hellenistic and Roman Periods from Alexander the Great Down to the Reign of Constantine (323 B.C.–A.D. 337)* (Ann Arbor, MI: University of Michigan Press, 2002), 176–77.

and the epigraphic database even cross-references them. There is no attempt, however, to resolve the discrepancy in dates. The database is at least explicit in offering the dates according to the publications, when no date is given in IG. The discrepancy between dates in this case is dependent on disagreement over both the archaeological context of the mosaic and the letter forms.[18] In such cases the researcher will have to assess the arguments and offer a reasonable judgment on the possibilities. Therefore, some of the principles used for determining a date where none is offered whatsoever will come into play.

4. Reading the inscription

a. Understanding conventions

There are agreed conventions for the presentation of ancient texts that were established in 1931 and have been used in subsequent publications.[19] This system, known as the Leiden Conventions, specifies a method of marking lacunae, scribal corrections, emendations, doubtful letters, and so on. One will thus find marks such as these amid the Greek transcriptions:

<αβγ>   Letters omitted by the scribe, added by modern editor
\αβγ/   Text inserted above the line in antiquity by a scribe
/αβγ\   Text inserted below the line in antiquity by a scribe

These symbols are familiar to anyone working regularly in the field and therefore are not explained in every edition. Indeed, for those using the online databases, there is no obvious direct link to them, even when a list of abbreviations exists.[20] Understandably, publications from before 1931 may use different conventions, and electronic editions based on them could still use different systems. However, this standard does allow for easier reading of transcriptions once the scholar is familiar with them.[21] Consultation of any introduction to papyri or an online search for the Leiden Conventions will be sufficient for inscriptions.[22]

---

18. See chapter 5, 1.g.

19. B. A. van Groningen, "Projet d'unification des systèmes de signes critiques," *ChrEg* 7 (1932): 262–69.

20. For papyri, a page of conventions is available, but without a link to it from other pages [Online: papyri.info/conventions.html]. My thanks to Chris Fresch for discovering this one.

21. The situation is improving even more with EpiDoc, a collaborative team of scholars who have drawn up an agreed system of guidelines and tools for encoding editions of ancient documents.

22. A helpful English version of the Conventions can be found in E. G. Turner, *Greek Papyri: An Introduction* (Oxford: Clarendon, 1980), 187–88.

b. Restorations

Particular care should be taken regarding restorations. Some restorations are feasible since the use of set phrases in many inscriptions allows for easy reconstruction. The noun ἴνδαλμα 'form, appearance' (Jer 27:39; Wis 17:3), for example, appears to be first attested in the Septuagint, even though it is a derivative of the verb ἰνδάλλομαι 'to appear, seem,' known since Homer. The noun's occasional appearance in inscriptions, therefore, offers hope for understanding the word better or finding earlier attestations. However, the one pre-Christian example (early fourth century B.C.E.) is an epitaph from Attica that contains significant reconstruction:

[κάλλος nomen νεότη]τα τε γαῖα δέδε[κται]·
[ἴνδαλμα ψυχῆς πολυδέ]γμονι δ᾽ ἐστὶ παρ᾽Ἄ[ιδηι]·(SEG 30:264.1–2)

This is the restoration by Peek, who draws the phrase ἴνδαλμα ψυχῆς from the much later IG II² 12142, a third-century C.E. inscription.[23] The *editio princeps* (IG II² 11356) left the majority of the damaged parts without restoration, and the first attempt at restoration offered quite a different reading:

[σύγγαμον ἐνθάδε σεῖο, Μακάρ]τατε, γαῖα δέδε[κται]
[Κλειταγόρην?, ψυχὴ πολυδέ]γμονι δ᾽ ἐστὶ παρ᾽Ἄι[δηι]²⁴

This example is demonstrative of how varied reconstructions can be and how misleading is the consultation of one edition alone. In the databases the explanations for editorial amendments or restorations are not offered, and therefore one must consult the published edition upon which it is based.

c. Checking the sources

It is necessary to check as many editions as possible of any sources and compare the editions with the readings given in the databases. The typing of text into the databases might not always have been reliable, and unclear cases should particularly be checked. The editions of texts, especially inscriptions, will often not provide translations, but one should rely on one's own knowledge of Greek to assess the text. Publications likewise might not be accurate in accents or the readings of words, and one

---

23. W. Peek, *Attische Versinschriften* (ASAW 69.2; Berlin: Akademie-Verlag, 1980), 51 no. 59.
24. A. Wilhelm, "Bemerkungen zu den attischen Grabinschriften I.G.II²," *ZPE* 29 (1978): 57–90 (77–78); SEG 28:323.

should make one's own judgment. Evans points to the papyrus example in P.Col.Zen. I 10 (TM 1731) of βουλη, which is of course without accents in the papyrus but which the editors in the index marked as the noun βουλή.[25] This reading was taken up by the PHI CD-Rom and the Duke Data Bank of Documentary Papyri. However, Evans shows that it should not be read as the noun, but accented as the second person singular subjunctive of the verb βούλομαι with loss of final iota (βούλῃ).[26] Sadly, despite Evans's article being cited in the metadata of APIS and Trismegistos, ten years on and the text in the Duke Data Bank has not been corrected. A different example is the appearance of an apparently unique word ἐξαρισκεύεσθαι in P.Hamb. 2.182.6 (TM 4336), which the editors struggle to explain as a lexicalization of ῥίσκος 'sarcophagus' denoting 'to transport.' In reality an *iota* has probably simply been written instead of an *epsilon* and we should interpret this as a derivative of middle of the verb ἐξαρέσκω 'to satisfy.'[27]

One should bear in mind that the editors of documentary texts were aiming to produce a corpus within a reasonable length of time and some-times could only make a decision with limited resources. They were not concerned with the lexicography of any particular word, and did not have the luxury of a lexicographer to investigate every occurrence of a word. Furthermore, since the original publication new data might have come to light to clarify a particular text. For those at the beginning of the twen-tieth century they were encountering the Greek in these sources for the first time and had to come to decisions without the century or more of experience that we now have of this type of Greek.

5. Analyzing the data

Finally, when analyzing the lexical samples, there are further issues to be noted.

a. Excluding duplicates

The online editions often have duplicate versions of the same in-scriptions, since each printed publication in which it appears is digitized. Editions in SEG in particular are often republications of other versions and therefore create duplicates. The results of lexical searches need to be sorted to remove such cases. At times, the republication might include a

---

25. T. V. Evans, "A Note on βουλή in P.Col.Zen. I 10," *ZPE* 145 (2003): 246–48.

26. This is how it is interpreted in the translation by J. L. White, *Light from Ancient Letters* (Foundations and Facets; Philadelphia, PA: Fortress, 1986), 37.

27. So J. K. Aitken, "Rhetoric and Poetry in Greek Ecclesiastes," *BIOSCS* 38 (2005): 55–78 (67 n. 30).

modified text if the editor has proposed a different reading from his predecessor, such that it is not always clear if it is the same inscription or not. Such differences between editions of the same inscription, however, draw attention to the problems of reading the text.

b. Pseudo-inscriptions

The Packhum database includes what one might call pseudo-inscriptions. These are inscriptions that are no longer extant but have been recorded by ancient authors or modern epigraphists. In the case of the ancient authors, it cannot be known whether the inscription existed, or if it did, whether the wording has been modified by the author or not. An example is the Adulis Inscription (OGIS 54), dated to 240 B.C.E. (reign of Ptolemy III, on the third Syrian war), which is known only from the Christian Topography (2.58–59) of Cosmas Indicopleustes (sixth century C.E.).[28] Its authenticity is open to question and therefore it should not be used as prime evidence.

c. Translation

Translation is always an essential element of lexicographic work. To assist in translating difficult inscriptions it is helpful to find other attempts to translate the text. They do not always exist or are not easy to find. A promising sign is the new online version of the *Inscriptiones Graecae* (IG) volumes that is currently being developed, which provides translations into German.[29] It is a digital edition of the Greek text from those volumes (starting with IG IX 1^2 4, published in 2001) along with a parallel German translation, although it is planned to include other languages in time.

---

28. See S. Burstein, *The Hellenistic Age from the Battle of Ipsos to the Death of Kleopatra VII* (Translated Documents of Greece and Rome 3; Cambridge: Cambridge University Press, 1985), 125–26.

29. IG online: telota.bbaw.de/ig/.

CHAPTER 4

New Words

In the following chapters some examples will illustrate the benefit of incorporating inscriptions into a lexicographic study of the Septuagint, and indeed of the New Testament. Each one is demonstrative of the distinctive contribution that inscriptions can make. In many of the examples the word falls into more than one category. A word, for example, that is a new attestation of the form in extrabiblical Greek inevitably also provides evidence of its semantics and could also contribute to our understanding of its geographical distribution. It is for convenience and illustration that they have been allocated to one chapter or another.

This chapter introduces words that are extremely rare or previously unattested, since with these we can see at once the importance of the new data. Where a word is not previously attested outside of the biblical and related writings, it is no surprise to find it now appearing in the sources. Chance survival only allows partial insight into the word groups of antiquity, and many words can be seen as standard formations of well-attested cognate forms. Greek, as any language, had particular methods of forming nouns and verbs through the regular addition of prefixes and suffixes, and we can expect certain words, though not attested outside biblical Greek, to have been part of the normal vocabulary.[1] While such formation also allows for authors to create new words within the system of the language,[2] documentary evidence indicates that we should not take that as the default option for Septuagint words. The sources increasingly show that the Septuagint reflects standard Koine of the time such that where a word is as yet unattested it need not be presumed that it is a new formation.

Ever since the time of Deissmann, the identification of words previously unattested has been an important contribution of documentary

---

1. These issues are succinctly discussed in J. A. L. Lee, *A Lexical Study of the Septuagint Version of the Pentateuch* (SBLSCS 14; Chico, CA: Scholars Press, 1983), 47–50.

2. See J. K. Aitken, "Neologisms: A Septuagint Problem," in *Interested Readers: Essays on the Hebrew Bible in Honor of David J. A. Clines* (ed. J. K. Aitken, J. M. S. Clines, and C. M. Maier; Atlanta, GA: SBL, 2013), 315–29.

sources. Ancient Greek was receptive to the creation of new words. Much of John Lee's influential *Lexical Study of the Septuagint* is focused upon innovations, classed as new semantic developments (in existing words), new formations (on existing stems), new words (primarily loanwords or dialectal), and innovation through obsolescence.[3] Lee takes a restrained approach to the identification of new words. He notes throughout that even if a word is not attested outside of the Septuagint, there is no reason why it has to be unique to the Septuagint, given the ability in Greek to create new formations from existing stems. He thus points to πλινθεία 'brick-making,' only attested in the Septuagint (Exod 1:14, etc.) and Josephus (*Ant.* 2.289) but one of many derivatives of πλίνθος, and to διασάφησις 'explanation, interpretation,' only attested in the Septuagint (Gen 40:8) but a normal formation of the verb διασαφέω, well attested in papyri (but see now chapter 5 §1.d). Accordingly for these he concludes that there is no reason to doubt that they are "normal Greek."[4] In one case his questioning has now been vindicated. It has been common to view προσήλυτος as a new formation in the Septuagint to translate the Hebrew noun גר with the meaning 'convert.'[5] This was doubted by Lee, who saw the Greek as a natural derivative of the verb προσέρχομαι and therefore a word that might have existed but simply disappeared from our record.[6] This supposition has proven to be correct by the discovery of a non-Jewish documentary papyrus from the third century B.C.E. with the very word denoting an 'immigrant.'[7] It is a salutary reminder to be wary of evidence from silence.

As discussed earlier (chapter 1), the lexicons frequently mark words that are not attested in Greek before the Septuagint or before the second century B.C.E. The high number of such words is representative of the extent to which Septuagint Greek is drawn from contemporary Koine rather than the higher literary language. There is little subtlety though in such marking. It does not distinguish between types of formation—the addition of a prefix, a compound word, a derivation from an existing noun or verb—and semantic innovation—an existing word adopting a new meaning. As it is a simple system of marking that aims at brevity in a lexicon, it is unable to give an account of the innovation. If the word is attested at least in the third century B.C.E. then it is certainly not an innovation of the

---

3. Lee, *Lexical Study*, 53–84, 85–113, 114–17, 118–28. See too his general discussion of the issue of new words (40–44).

4. Lee, *Lexical Study*, 47.

5. The classic study is W. C. Allen, "On the Meaning of ΠΡΟΣΗΛΥΤΟΣ in the Septuagint," *Expositor* 4.10 (1894): 264–75.

6. J. A. L. Lee, "Equivocal and Stereotyped Renderings in the LXX," *RB* 87 (1980): 104–17 (112–13).

7. D. M. Moffitt and C. J. Butera, "P.Duk.Inv. 727: A Dispute with 'Proselytes' in Egypt," *ZPE* 177 (2011): 201–6.

Septuagint. Even a later attestation might be an indication that the word is not an innovation. The relative dating of individual Septuagint books, spanning some centuries, also needs to be taken into account. Rather than choosing an arbitrary third- or second-century date, evidence will be considered if it sheds light on a particular book in which a word is found. Words attested in either third- or second-century B.C.E. sources should be sufficient to show that the words are not new formations in the Septuagint.

The lexicons that mark such words are admittedly not offering any conclusions on such data. However, they can contribute to the picture of a distinctive form of Greek in the Septuagint, and therefore a nuanced understanding of such new words needs to be borne in mind by the reader. In addition to the twenty examples in this chapter, we could add a further set of words discussed in later chapters under different categories: ἀδελφότης 'brotherhood,' διασάφησις 'explanation,' ἔναντι 'in front of,' εὐ(ε)ίλατος 'merciful,' εὐλογέω 'to praise,' καμηλοπάρδαλις 'giraffe,' ὀνοκένταυρος 'onocentaur,' and ὀνοματογραφία 'list.'

When considering poorly attested words, as the majority of these will be, care needs to be taken. The evidence will always be slight for poorly attested words, but one should aim for certain rather than speculative readings. This is particularly the case where there are reconstructions in the published editions of inscriptions. In 1 Kgdms 8:13 we find the feminine noun μαγείρισσα 'cook,' which, as noted by LSJ (1071), is only attested here in Greek sources. Given the existence of the common masculine equivalent μάγειρος, there is no reason, other than the social roles of women, why this noun would have been invented by the Septuagint translators. Tantalizingly there is an inscription from Carthage that could confirm this, but consultation of the inscription indicates that this is far from certain.

[— — —]ϲη μαγε[— — —]
[— — —]τος (ICKarth 2:768)

It is a Christian epitaph (of uncertain date), and thus the letters might comprise the occupation of the deceased, and suggestions have included μαγε[ίρισσα] as well as μαγε[ίραινα].[8] The latter word is also a feminine form of μάγειρος, and attested once only in literature.[9] There are few options as to how μαγε[might be reconstructed. Therefore it might well be μαγε[ίρισσα], but there is no certainty. A more problematic example is

---

8. L. Ennabli, *Les inscriptions funéraires chrétiennes de Carthage. par Liliane Ennabli. 2, La basilique de Mcidfa* (Collection de l'École française de Rome 62; Rome: École française de Rome, 1982), 332.

9. From the comic Pherecrates, as quoted in Athenaeus, *Deipnosophistae* 13.94.

the noun εὐδοκία, 'goodwill,' a variant of εὐδόκησις, particularly used of God in the Septuagint (Ps 5:13, etc.). Consultation of LSJ would suggest the Septuagint represents the first uses of this word and that it has an influence on later Christian literature (e.g., Luke 2:14). Both the verb εὐδοκέω and the noun εὐδόκησις are themselves only attested from the time of Polybius. However, there is one possible instance of εὐδοκία in a dedication on a statue. The Phokians dedicated to Apollo at Delphi this statue of Xanthippos of Phokis, the son of Ampharetos, who had liberated Elateia (dated to 284–281 B.C.E.):

> τοὔνεκα καὶ Φωκεῖς δεκάκις, ξένε, ταγὸν ἔθεντο,
> τόν γε μετ᾽ εὐδο[κί]α[ς] πάντες ἐπευχόμ[εν]οι. (FD III
> 4:220+221.11–12)[10]
>
> Therefore, stranger, the Phokians elected him *tagus* ten times, and all offered him pray[er]s with good[wi]l[l].

This would seem to be a fitting equivalent to the use in the Psalms, but the reading is damaged, and quite different alternative transcriptions have been suggested: τόν γε μετ᾽ εὐδόξ[ο]υ or τόν γε μετ᾽ εὐλο[γίας]. Both of these alternatives are built upon words already established in the language and are therefore more likely than the reading εὐδοκία.

It is hoped that any such doubtful cases have been eliminated and only confident attestations are offered. The one instance where there is some reconstruction of the reading is in the case of διασάφησις, to be discussed under semantics (chapter 5, 1.d), but even then there are few possible alternatives.

A second issue is how far to indicate words that existed earlier but with a different sense. As an example, the noun παραδρομή appears twice in the Septuagint, once in an obscure use (Cant 7:6) perhaps to indicate the train of trailing hair, and once in an established usage of a retinue or group of accompanying people (2 Macc 3:28). LSJ (1309) provides examples from Plutarch and Posidonius as best examples, but does also include the sense ἐν παραδρομῇ 'cursorily.' A similar use is found in a mid-third century B.C.E. law from Kandahar:

> καὶ τοῦτο ἐμ παραδρομῆι οἱ λοιποὶ ἡγεῖνται (IGExtrEast 292.11)
>
> and the rest consider this a trivial matter (lit. 'in passing' or 'as a supplement')[11]

---

10. So too SEG 14:461; Syll.³ 361C.

11. Canali De Rossi, IGExtrEast 190 translates the phrase as "trascurabile"; Merkelach and Stauber by "nebensächlich" (*Jenseits des Euphrat: griechische Inschriften. Ein epigra-*

The inscription does not provide a precise parallel to the odd Septuagint uses, but attests at least to an earlier use of the word. Such examples are nonetheless notable for their attestation to the existence of the word by the time of the Septuagint, and therefore worthy of recording.

1. γένημα

It is clear from consultation of LSJ that the spelling γένημα 'produce, of the fruits of the earth' with a single ν (cf. γέννημα) is known at the same time as the LXX Pentateuch. LSJ cite P.Rev. 24.15 (TM 8859) from the third century B.C.E., which had been published in 1896.[12] Deissmann had already recorded a number of examples from the Roman period,[13] and observed that the earliest one known in his time was P.Petr. 1.16 (TM 7633), but there can now be found as many as 250 examples before the first century. The first literary occurrence is in Polybius, but the epigraphic material allows the word to be traced back to the third century B.C.E.[14] This is in accord with the papyri, and broadens the evidence of this form of the word at the time of the earliest Septuagint translations.

2. δεκαμηνιαῖος

It is easy to imagine that some might wish to speak of something being of ten months in age or duration, and therefore use the adjective δεκαμηνιαῖος. Although this word is found in Wisdom of Solomon, and it is conceivable that the author could have invented it, it would seem un-likely given the versatility of the adjectival ending, and the appearance of the adjective in later authors. In Wis 7:2 Solomon describes his own birth:

1 . . . καὶ ἐν κοιλίᾳ μητρὸς ἐγλύφην σὰρξ
2 δεκαμηνιαίῳ χρόνῳ παγεὶς ἐν αἵματι ἐκ σπέρματος ἀνδρὸς καὶ ἡδονῆς ὕπνῳ συνελθούσης.

---

phisches Lesebuch. Zusammengestellt, übersetzt und erklärt von Reinhold Merkelbach und Josef Stauber [Munich: Saur, 2005], 31).

12. *Revenue Laws of Ptolemy Philadelphus* (ed. B. P. Grenfell; Oxford: Clarendon, 1896), 201 edict 13.

13. G. A. Deissmann, *Bible Studies: Contributions, Chiefly from Papyri and Inscriptions, to the History of the Language, the Literature, and the Religion of Hellenistic Judaism and Primitive Christianity* (Edinburgh: T. & T. Clark, 1909), 109–10, 184.

14. SEG 37:1003[2] (shortly after 214/3 B.C.E.?, Sardis); ISardis 7,1.1 (c. 200 B.C.E.); ISardis 7,1.2; IMiletMcCabe 61.41 (183/164 B.C.E.); IMiletMcCabe 45 II–III.3 (c. 165 B.C.E.); CIG 3546.40 (pre 149/150 C.E., Pergamon); IMylasa 128.3 (Hellenistic); IMylasa 127.3; IMylasa 51.29; IMylasa 41.23; IScM III 26.8 (c. mid-first century B.C.E., Scythia Minor); TAM II 245.10 (Roman period, Lycia); IG V 2.515B.14 (after 14 C.E., Lykosoura); Agora 16 337.38 (first century C.E., Athens).

In my mother's womb I was fashioned into flesh for a period of ten months, impacted with blood from the seed of a man and the pleasure that comes with sleep.

LSJ (376) notes two examples of δεκαμηνιαῖος, one denoting a period of time (χρόνος, Plutarch, *Numa* 12), and in similar fashion to Wisdom describing the age of a child in the mother's womb (Alexander of Aphrodisias, *Problems* 1.40, a third-century C.E. philosopher). In antiquity pregnancy was thought to last ten months, perhaps based on a lunar calendar. A variant form δεκάμηνος is more widely attested. The Plutarch example is enough to suggest that it is a literary word, presumably rare owing to its absence in everyday speech. Epigraphic material provides an earlier example in an aretalogy or "self-predication" of Isis, dated to the first century B.C.E.:[15]

ἐγὼ γυναικὶ δεκαμηνιαῖον βρέφος εἰς φῶς ἐξενεγκεῖν ἔταξα. (IKyme 41.19)

I prescribed for a woman to bring forth into the daylight a ten-month-old child.

This text is from Cyme in Aeolis, although the opening of the inscription declares that is has been been copied from a stele at Memphis (l. 3: τάδε ἐγράφηι ἐκ τῆς στήλης τῆς ἐν Μέμφει). The same Isis hymn, in a more damaged form, is also found in Mygdonia, Thessalonika, from the first or second century C.E. (IG X 2.1 254). Both the Isis hymn and Alexander of Aphrodisias provide the same context of childbirth as that found in Wisdom, while Plutarch offers the same collocation with χρόνος.

This example has a particular significance since it is one of the thirty-five or more words in Wisdom that Winston has recorded as not appearing before the first century C.E.[16] His data have been used by many to confirm a first-century C.E. dating of the book, although the redating of the epigraphy means that the word δεκαμηνιαῖος can be seen to have existed earlier than the first century. One wonders how many more from Winston's examples require reexamination.

3. διατήρησις

The Bible prescribes the reservation of certain offerings, including the manna in the wilderness:

---

15. This example was already known to D. Winston, *The Wisdom of Solomon: A New Translation with Introduction and Commentary* (AB 43; Garden City, NY: Doubleday, 1979), 163, but he understood it to be first century C.E.

16. Winston, *Wisdom of Solomon*, 22 and n. 33.

ἀποθήσεις αὐτὸ ἐναντίον τοῦ θεοῦ εἰς διατήρησιν εἰς τὰς γενεὰς ὑμῶν. (Exod 16:33)

You shall place it before God as a keepsake for your descendants.

διατήρησις appears five times in the Pentateuch (Exod 16:33, 34; Num 17:25; 18:8; 19:9), and in four of these in the construction εἰς διατήρησιν (for MT לְמִשְׁמֶרֶת). In each case objects are set aside and reserved or placed in safekeeping for ritual use.[17] Elsewhere in Exodus the Hebrew is translated by ἀποθήκη 'deposit' (Exod 16:32).[18]

Remarkably, the same construction appears in the regulations concerning the cult of Zeus Akraios, found carved on two fragments of a white marble plaque from Thessalia (Magnesia).

καὶ τὸ ἐκ τούτων [διάφορον] | γενόμενον διδόναι εἰς διατήρησιν τῶι ἱερεῖ τοῦ Διὸς τοῦ Ἀκραίου . . . (SEG 25:687.7–8)[19]

and it is necessary to give whatever [difference] of this money for keeping in the temple of Zeus Akraios

Sokolowski adopts the reading of his predecessor, although he has doubts about the subject of διατήρησις, noting the alternative reading of ἀγόμενον for γενόμενον.[20] Irrespective of the syntax, the inscription is dated to the Hellenistic period, thereby providing not only a near contemporary attestation of the word, but a very close semantic equivalent.

4. διορθωτής

In Wis 7:15 God is described as the corrector of the wise:

ὅτι αὐτὸς καὶ τῆς σοφίας ὁδηγός ἐστιν
καὶ τῶν σοφῶν διορθωτής.

For he himself is also the leader of wisdom
and the corrector of the wise.

This term eventually becomes a technical term in manuscript editing, and the corrector of a codex can identify himself as such in the colophon,[21]

---

17. On the meaning of the Hebrew, see E. W. Davies, *Numbers* (NCBC; Grand Rapids, MI: Eerdmans, 1995), 186–87.

18. Noted by A. Le Boullec and P. Sandevoir, *La Bible d'Alexandrie, 2: L'Exode* (Paris: Cerfs, 1989), 188.

19. The text was published as IG IX 2.1110, but was then republished with improved readings by F. Sokolowski, *Lois sacrées des cités grecques* (Travaux et mémoires 18; Paris: de Boccard, 1969), 171–72 no. 85.

20. *Lois sacrées*, 171.

21. T. Dorandi, "Korrekturzeichen," in *Der neue Pauly: Enzyklopädie der Antike* (16 vols.; ed. H. Cancik and H. Schneider; Stuttgart: Metzler, 1996–2003), 7: 759–60.

a use dating from at least the first century B.C.E. (Diodorus Siculus, *BH* 15.6). For its non-technical sense LSJ (434) gives Wisdom as the first example, followed by Plutarch (*Solon* 16) who describes Solon as the 'reformer of the constitution' (τῆς πολιτείας διορθωτήν). A cognate noun διορθωτήρ also exists, but is even rarer. It is, however, attested as early as 303–300 B.C.E. in an Arkadian inscription (IPArk 17 = IG V 2.357). As for διορθωτής it also appears early in reference to political reformers in the late third century B.C.E. (IGonnoi II 122). An earlier example might appear at the beginning of the third century but the reading is uncertain (IG XI 4 1028.frg.a1.2: διορθωταὶ).

The epigraphic evidence not only offers the earliest attestations for the word διορθωτής, and indeed for διορθωτήρ, but also offers hints as to its connotation. While the term also took on philosophical connotations (as in Epictetus, *Discourses* 3.7.1), it is largely used in political contexts from the third century B.C.E. onwards. Wisdom as a guide expressed in political terms would be important for a book addressed to rulers (Wis 1:1).[22]

5. δόκωσις

The noun δόκωσις 'furnishing with rafters, roofing' (LSJ 443) only appears in the Septuagint in the relatively late translation of Ecclesiastes.

ἐν ὀκνηρίαις ταπεινωθήσεται ἡ δόκωσις,
καὶ ἐν ἀργίᾳ χειρῶν στάξει ἡ οἰκία. (Eccl 10:18)

In sloth the roofing will be lowered
And in idle hands the house will drip.

The Greek ἡ δόκωσις translates Hebrew הַמְּקָרֶה, a noun cognate with קוֹרָה "beam" (Gen 19:8; 4 Kgdms 6:2, 5; etc.).[23] The parallelism with οἰκία in the Greek (Hebrew בַּיִת) indicates it is either part of a building or a whole building, but the few occurrences of the noun outside the Septuagint suggest the meaning is reasonably well established.[24] Judging from the citations in LSJ δόκωσις is attested only in Roman period literature

---

22. G. Scarpat discusses at length the many connotations of the term (*Libro della Sapienza: testo, traduzione, introduzione e commento* [3 vols.; Brescia: Paideia, 1989–99], 2: 35–39). C. Larcher merely wishes to tone down the strength of the word (*Le livre de la sagesse, ou, La sagesse de Salomon* [Paris: Gabalda, 1983–85], 2: 465–66).

23. A. Schoors, *The Preacher Sought to Find Pleasing Words: A Study of the Language of Qoheleth* (2 vols.; Leuven: Peeters, 1992–2004), 2: 461.

24. H. Debel and E. Verbeke, "The Greek Rendering of Hebrew *Hapax Legomena* in the Book of Qoheleth," in *XIV Congress of the International Organization for Septuagint and Cognate Studies, Helsinki, 2010* (ed. M. K. H. Peters; Atlanta, GA: SBL, 2013), 313–31 (328–29) propose that since the Greek word is a *hapax* in the LXX, the meaning of the

(Plutarch, *Moralia* [*Against Colotes*] 1112e; Sextus Empiricus, *Outlines of Pyrrhonism* 3.99; *Against the Mathematicians* 9.343) and one papyrus also from that period (P.Oxy. 14.1648.60 [TM 29012], second century C.E.).[25] This might be no surprise since the translation of Ecclesiastes is usually deemed to be one of the latest in the Septuagint, in at least the first century C.E., owing to its proximity in method to the second-century translator Aquila. The word could then be called upon in support of a late dating for Ecclesiastes.

There has been one papyrus published additional to that recorded in LSJ that contains the word. In a petition (P.Tebt. 3.1.781 [TM 5369], c. 164 B.C.E.) a priest complains that rebels have attacked his shrine. They inflict some damage to the temple:

καὶ ἔτι | [δο]κώσεις τινὰς κα[τα]σπασάντων

and also to[rn] down some of the [boa]rding (ll. 11–12)

It seems clear that the meaning is boards, used in an architectural structure, and the date of this papyrus takes us back to an earlier time for the use of the word. An inscription, however, once more provides us with the earliest example, and indeed one considerably earlier than these references would imply. In a corpus of inscriptions from the eastern Greek islands, we read in an Aeolic inscription of building supplies to be sent from Lesbos, for the building of a stoa:

τὸ δὲ ξύλομα {ξύλωμα}[26] Χίαν δ[ό]|[κ]ωσιν (IG XII 2.14.9–10)

Chian wood for ro[of]ing

Although the inscription is undated, other inscriptions in the collection seem to be early Hellenistic, and therefore Heisserer dates this one to c. 300–275 B.C.E.[27]

Greek could be derived from the Hebrew meaning. They make no reference to extrabiblical Greek evidence.

25. Appearances in the Church Fathers are with reference to the Ecclesiastes passage.

26. See R. Hodot, "Notes critiques sur le corpus épigraphique de Lesbos," *Etudes d'Archéologie classique* 5 (1976): 17–81 (23) for the reading ξύλωμα in line 9.

27. A. J. Heisserer, "Observations on 'IG' XII 2, 10 and 11," *ZPE* 74 (1988): 111–32 (132). C. Williams, "Hellenistic and Roman Buildings in the Mediaeval Walls of Mytilene," *Phoenix* 38 (1984): 31–76 (36, n. 4), notes that although the date of "4th c. B.C.?" was originally given to this inscription, no justification is provided for this estimation (L. B. Holland, F. W. Householder, and R. L. Scranton, *A Sylloge of Greek Building Inscriptions* [unpublished manuscript, ASCS library, Athens], 1009, 2064 no. 195). Hodot, "Notes critiques," 59, observes that Hiller proposed a third- or second-century date, but in the end favored the later date on the basis of itacism. However, by comparison with other inscriptions, it appears to be a third-century phenomenon.

In terms of meaning, we perhaps can nuance the translations so far suggested. LSJ's 'furnishing with rafters, roofing'[28] might be influenced by the medieval lexicons in which δόκωσις is glossed as στέγη 'roof' (Hesychius, Photius, and others). This has certainly motivated Grenfell and Hunt's translation of the papyrus:

πεπράκ(ασι) τὰ ὑπάρχ(οντα) αὐτῃ (read αὐταῖς) | φορτία καὶ
δόκωσιν καὶ τὰ συνῳκοδομημ(ένα) | βαφικὰ ἐργαστήρια (P.Oxy.
14.1648.59–61)

. . . have sold the produce and roof and dyeing-workshops constructed jointly[29]

In Plutarch (*Moralia* § 1112e) a δόκωσις is defined as a δοκός 'beam,' while Sextus Empiricus, in the midst of a discussion that nothing exists other than the parts of which it is made, suggests that a δόκωσις is nothing other than the 'beams laid out' (παρὰ τὰ δεδοκωμένα *Outlines of Pyrrhonism* 3.99). It appears from these authors that a δόκωσις can be identified by the beams that are essential to it. In the inscription from Mytilene the products being transported are the beams themselves for the construction of the rafters. The papyrus from Oxyrhynchus could be interpreted in a number of possible ways and therefore is not to be relied upon. In Sextus Empiricus the word seems to portray something composed of beams and therefore is most likely the roofing that displays the rafters. In other cases (IG XII 2.14; P.Tebt. 3.1.781; Plutarch) it appears to be the beams themselves for the roofing. Naturally, in antiquity roofs would have been made up of beams, and therefore rafters or beamed roof, in which the beams were visible, would be most appropriate.[30] A 'roof' does not convey this sense in contemporary English.

6. δορκάδιον

The noun δορκάδιον (Isa 13:14), diminutive of δορκάς 'a kind of deer' (LSJ 445), has already been well documented. LEH (160: "neol.?") and GELS (176) correctly indicate the word is not attested before the time of the Septuagint. It is nonetheless contemporary with it and therefore an example of a word that is not strictly new at the time. It is known from a mid-third-century B.C.E. papyrus (P.Cair.Zen 3.59429.12 [TM 1069]) in which a goatherd by the name of Hermias records his purchase of a small

---

28. There is no entry in the word before the ninth edition of Liddell and Scott.
29. B. P. Grenfell and A. S. Hunt, *The Oxyrhynchus Papyri, Part XIV* (London: Egypt Exploration Society, 1920), 86.
30. See now the definition given in the *DGE* 1142: "*viguería, trabazón de vigas y esp. techumbre, tejado de tablas*" ("beams, interlocking beams and esp. roofing, roof boards").

deer (δορκάδιον).[31] LSJ had already indicated the third-century origin of the word by reference to IG XI 2.203A.10. In that case the object is a piece of jewelry, but in the shape of a small deer and therefore still attesting to the same use.

7. ἐκλοχίζω

Until recently, the word ἐκλοχίζω (attested only in Cant 5:10) appeared to be a neologism of the Septuagint. While obviously a derivative of the noun λόχος 'a body of people,' as with the similar denominative λοχίζω 'to lie in wait' or 'to distribute,' there was no attestation outside of the Septuagint occurrence. Accordingly LSJ only provided the Septuagint as a source (512), and the lexicons recorded it as a neologism. In Canticles the verb describes the beloved:

ἀδελφιδός μου λευκὸς καὶ πυρρός ἐκλελοχισμένος ἀπὸ μυριάδων.

My beloved is white and reddish, selected from tens of thousands.

Supporting epigraphic evidence had been known for more than a century, but had not received attention in a lexicographic context.[32] In an inscription from Hermopolis Magna in Egypt (SB 1:4206.239 [TM 7099]), from the first century B.C.E. (between 80 and 69 B.C.E.), the verb appears in a list of officials, and is used to describe the royal swordsmen:

ἐγλελοχισμένοι μαχαιροφό(ροι) βα(σιλικοί)

the royal select swordsmen

It appears that the verb, in both instances a perfect passive participle, is a technical term to denote specially selected for a purpose, perhaps with a military connotation as could be implied by the root λοχός. It is possible in Cant 5:10 that the qualification ἀπὸ μυριάδων, which could denote a cohort of troops, prompted the translator to choose a word with such a military connotation, although without further examples we cannot be sure. As noted by De Crom, the Greek translates the Hebrew passive participle דָּגוּל 'distinguished,' a verb whose cognates often appear in military contexts.[33]

It is clear from the inscription that the LXX translator did not invent the word, but chose one in parlance at the time. It is striking that in both

---

31. LEH gives a reference to Preisigke, presumably using this papyrus as the reason for placing a question mark next to "neol."

32. First published in J. G. Milne, *Greek Inscriptions* (Service des Antiquités de l'Égypte: Catalogue géneral des antiquités égyptiennes du Musée du Caire; Oxford: Oxford University Press, 1905), no. 9296. It has now been recorded in *DGE* 1377.

33. D. De Crom, "The Lexicon of LXX Canticles and Greco-Roman Papyri," *ZAW* 124 (2012): 255–62 (258–59).

cases the perfect passive participle is found, and this further suggests that in this form the term was used in specific contexts. As it is usually assumed that the LXX translation of Canticles is relatively late, either the first century B.C.E. or C.E.,[34] then the LXX case is not earlier but in fact from the same period as the inscription. This example had already been noted by the present author,[35] but was overlooked in a discussion that focused exclusively on the papyri.[36]

8. ἔλασμα

In its condemnation of idolatry, Habakkuk summarizes the inherent foolishness in an idol:

καὶ αὐτό ἐστιν φαντασία, τοῦτο δέ ἐστιν ἔλασμα χρυσίου καὶ ἀργυρίου, καὶ πᾶν πνεῦμα οὐκ ἔστιν ἐν αὐτῷ. (Hab 2:19)

And it is a representation, that is, a beaten-out piece of gold and silver, and there is no breath in it. (NETS)

The noun ἔλασμα, a derivative of ἐλαύνω in its sense 'to strike,' is reasonably well attested from the first century C.E. onwards. LSJ (528) gives Philo as the earliest reference, while Montanari begins with Pausanias in the second century (651). The earliest reference can now be pushed back to the second century B.C.E. at the putative time of the translation of the Minor Prophets. In an inventory list from the sanctuary at Delos dated to 155/4 B.C.E. there is included one particular item:

ἔ]λασμα λαμπάδος σιδηρᾶς, ἀνάθεμα Τεισάνδρου (IDelos 1417.60)

p]late of an iron torch, dedication of Teisander

Similarly in another list

ἔ|[λ]ασμα λαμπάδος σιδηρᾶς· (IDelos 1443.C15)

p[l]ate of an iron torch

The diminutive ἐλασμάτιον, qualified by the adjective ἀργυροῦν, appears four times in the same set of inscriptions (IDelos 1443 *bis*, 1449; 1450),

---

34. See J. C. Treat, "Aquila, Field, and the Song of Songs," in *Origen's Hexapla and Fragments. Papers Presented at the Rich Seminar on the Hexapla, Oxford Centre for Hebrew and Jewish Studies, 25th [July]–3rd August 1994* (ed. A. Salvesen; TSAJ 58; Tübingen: Mohr Siebeck, 1998), 135–76 (135).

35. J. K. Aitken, "Context of Situation in Biblical Lexica," in *Foundations for Syriac Lexicography III: Colloquia of the International Syriac Language Project* (ed. J. Dyk and W. van Peursen; Perspectives on Syriac Linguistics 4; Piscataway, NJ: Gorgias, 2008), 181–201 (195–96).

36. De Crom, "Lexicon of LXX Canticles," 258–59.

all mid-second century B.C.E. It is unclear what an ἔλασμα is in these texts, perhaps the stand or holder for a torch. These inscriptions not only attest the existence of the word but show that it is an object dedicated at a shrine. LXX Habakkuk might then be condemning idols not merely as beaten-out metal but as dedicatory objects.

9. ἐπακουστός

ὦ ἄνδρες, πῶς οὐχ ὑπερισχύει ὁ βασιλεύς, ὅτι οὕτως ἐπακουστός ἐστιν; καὶ ἐσίγησεν. (1 Esd 4:12)

"O Gentlemen, how does not the king prove superior, since he is to be obeyed in this way?" And he fell silent.

The adjective ἐπακουστός 'to be listened to' has not been recorded as a neologism in Septuagint lexicons because, according to LSJ (605), it is first attested in Empedocles of the fifth century B.C.E. But Empedocles is only preserved in fragments quoted by later authors (Plutarch, Sextus Empiricus, and Diogenes Laertius), so caution should be exercised over the dating of his vocabulary. The word is only to be found elsewhere in literature in John Chrysostom, and therefore the one epigraphic example is significant. In a sacred law from Selinous in western Sicily, inscribed on a very large lead tablet (c. 450 B.C.E.), instructions are given on how to be purified of some sort of power called an *elasteros*:

αἴ τίς κα λêι ξενικὸν ê πατρôιον, ê 'πακουστὸν ê 'φορατὸν | ê καὶ χõντινα καθαίρεσθαι (col. B.7–8)

If anyone wishes to purify himself with respect to a foreign or ancestral one (sc. *elasteros*), either one that has been heard or one that has been seen, or anyone at all[37]

The word ἐπακουστός, here with the first letter elided to the preceding particle, probably refers to a supernatural manifestation, either heard or seen.[38] It confirms an early use of the adjective.

10. ἐπίγνωστος

The adjective ἐπίγνωστος 'known' (LSJ 627) is only found in LXX Job 18:19. Although no documentary evidence provides this word either, there is a late third-century or early second-century B.C.E. decree concerning

---

37. Text and translation of M. H. Jameson, D. R. Jordan, R. D. Kotansky, *A Lex Sacra from Selinous* (Greek, Roman, and Byzantine Monographs 11; Durham, NC: Duke University Press, 1993), 16–17.

38. Jameson et al., *Lex Sacra*, 44.

participation in the sanctuaries of Apollon and Herakles containing the adjective δυσεπίγνωστος 'hard to identify or find out' (Syll. 1023.9; SEG 54:748; Cos). This implies the simpler form ἐπίγνωστος might already have existed.

11. ἐπικατάρατος

The marking of ἐπικατάρατος 'accursed' as a "neol.?" (LEH 229) is no surprise when the cognate verb ἐπικαταράομαι also appears to be first attested in the Septuagint. LSJ (636) heads its entry for the adjective ἐπικατάρατος 'accursed' with the Septuagint (Gen 3:14)[39] followed by the New Testament. The remainder of the entry covers two inscriptions: "IG12(9).955 (Euboea); ταῖς ἀραῖς BMus.Inscr.918.6 (Halic.)." The date of IG XII 9.955 is uncertain, but an inscription with very similar wording, IG XII 9.1179, has been dated to the second century C.E. The second inscription in LSJ, from Halicarnassus (IBM 918 = CIG 2664), is a funerary inscription with curses against unauthorized burial and disturbing of the grave. It has been dated to the second or third century C.E.[40] In both cases the influence of Deuteronomic language is apparent and therefore they do not serve as independent sources.[41]

Other epigraphic evidence can now be cited that proves the use of the word as early as the third and maybe the fourth century B.C.E. There are two indisputable examples from the third century (IG IX 1² 1.148 and ILabraunda 8A). ILabraunda 8A (dated to 235 B.C.E.) from Caria in Asia Minor is a decree on the dedication of lands to Zeus with a warning against violation (ἐπικατάρατος καὶ ἄτιμος).[42] The fourth-century example has to be partially reconstructed, but enough of the word is preserved for reasonable confidence regarding its reading (ll. 13–15):

[ἐὰν δ]έ τις ταῦτα παραβαίνῃ ἢ ἄκυρα π[οιῇ,]
[ἐπικα]τάρατος ἔστω αὐτός τε καὶ τὰ τού[του]
[πάν]τα ἀπὸ τοῦ θεοῦ τούτου.[43]

---

39. There are a total of 45 occurrences in the Septuagint.

40. See B. F. Cook, *Greek Inscriptions* (Reading the Past; London: British Museum, 1987), 29.

41. See, e.g., L. Robert, "Malédictions funéraires grecques," *Comptes rendus des séances de l'Académie des Inscriptions et Belles-Lettres* 122 (1978): 241–89 (245); J. G. Gager, *Curse Tablets and Binding Spells from the Ancient World* (Oxford: Oxford University Press, 1992), 185; D. C. Lincicum, "Greek Deuteronomy's 'Fever and Chills' and Their Magical Afterlife," *VT* 58 (2008): 544–49 (547 n. 21).

42. See too IMylasa 941.4, a regulation concerning the temple of Zeus.

43. L. Robert, *Le sanctuaire de Sinuri près de Mylasa, I. Les inscriptions* (Mémoires de l'institut français d'archéologie de Stamboul 7; Paris: de Boccard, 1945), no. 73; corrections in *Hellenica* 7: 63–64; S. Hornblower, *Mausolus* (Oxford: Clarendon, 1982), 365 (M5).

[If] anyone transgresses this or [act]s without authority, may both he and [al]l his property be [cur]sed by this god.

The warding off of violators through the threat of being cursed by a god is a close parallel to the Septuagint usage.

12. ἐπίποκος

The adjective ἐπίποκος 'covered with wool, woolly', a derivative of the regular noun πόκος 'wool, fleece,' is only attested in the Lucianic version of 4 Kgdms 3:4. LSJ (652) notes it as uncertain in the Septuagint owing to its late recension, and invites comparison with GDI 3731.6, an inscription from Cos. They do not make clear whether the word is in that inscription or what the date is. It is in fact a third-century B.C.E. inscription (cf. SEG 49:1102) and therefore older than the Septuagint, containing the phrase ὄϊν] ἐπίποκον τελέ|[αν "per]fect woolly [sheep" (lines 6–7). The word is also partially reconstructed in another inscription from Cos in the expression ὄι τελέωι ἐπι|[πόκωι "a perfect woo[lly] sheep" (IKosHerzog 8 BIII.1.6–7; c. 270–260 B.C.E.).[44] The reconstruction is probable given the use of the same adjective as in the other inscription and the reference to a sheep.

13. ἐξάλειψις

It is curious how epigraphic data can easily be overlooked or discounted in discussions. This appears to be the case with ἐξάλειψις (Ezek 9:6; Mic 7:11), for which LSJ (583) provides evidence from an early inscription but distinguishes the sense from the Septuagint use. Thus, we find 'whitewashing' as the sense given in reference to the walls of a dressing room (ἀποδυτήριον) in the bathhouse, recorded on a third-century B.C.E. (247/246 B.C.E.) inscription from Delphi (*BCH* 23.566 = CID 2:139; cf. CID 4:57). The meaning in the Septuagint is given separately as 'blotting out, destruction.'[45] The meanings are different but clearly related—whitewashing the walls obliterates whatever was beneath it. The inscription testifies to the use of the word, if not in precisely the same context.

14. ἱματιοφύλαξ

A certain obsolescence of the English language appears in dictionary entries for ἱματιοφύλαξ. For the noun ἱματιοφύλαξ LSJ (829) only provides one reference, LXX 4 Kgdms 22:14, but its gloss 'keeper of the wardrobe' is derived from the KJV translation of the Hebrew. A 'wardrobe' in the time of the KJV denoted the room or chamber in which clothes were kept,

---

44. See also SEG 28:699(3); SEG 47:1277(1).

45. Cf. K. Hauspie, "Neologisms in the Septuagint of Ezekiel," *JNSL* 27 (2001): 17–37.

and this sense was still possible by the time of LSJ, but is now obsolete in English, conveying instead the sense of a cabinet. The lexicons (LEH 288; GELS 341) have persevered nonetheless with LSJ's definition, although Montanari's 'guardarobiere' (946) is more open to interpretation. It appears that the ἱματιοφύλαξ was responsible for the priestly vestments or the royal robes (cf. 4 Kgdms 10:22). The word only appears in a few church fathers, influenced by the biblical passage.

The likelihood of the word existing in Greek is supported by the cognate noun ἱματιοφυλάκιον appearing in an inscription and in two papyri, the earlier from the third century C.E. (SB 8:9921.10–11 [TM 31999]). From Perge in Pampylia a dedication inscription (81–96 C.E.) records:

τὸ ἐν τῷ ἱματιοφυλακίῳ τῶν | ποικίλων κειόνων δωδεκάσστυλον | 10 καὶ τοὺς πρὸ αὐ[τ]οῦ μέσους τέσσαρας κεί|ονας ἐκ τῶν ἰδίων ἀνέθηκε καὶ καθιέρω|σε (IPerge 60.8–12)

(Cn.Postumius Cornutus) established and dedicated from his own funds in the clothes storage room a twelve-column colonnade of polychrome pillars,[46] and the four middle pillars in front of [i]t

Herrmann draws comparison with the verb in Lucian's *Hippias* 8 (τὰς κοινὰς τῶν ἱματιοφυλακούντων κατασκευάς) and with the expression περί τε τῆς | φυλακῆς [τῶν ἱ]ματίων in an inscription from Pergamon.

15. κυρίευσις

The noun κυρίευσις is only found in the "Lucianic" version or "A text" of Esther, Addition F8 (GELS 419, which references the passage as Esth 7:56) and accordingly cannot be found in LEH.[47] The complexities of the relationship of this version to its Hebrew *Vorlage*, if there was one,[48] do not allow for sure conclusions on what Hebrew word the Greek might be translating.[49]

---

46. Following P. Herrmann, "Epigraphische Notizen: 18. ἱματιοφυλάκιον. 19. Stiftung des M. Feridius P. f. 20. Fragment einer Gladiatoreninschrift," *EA* 31 (1999): 31–34 (31–32), the polychrome pillars are translated as if part of the colonnade rather than referring back to the clothes room (translation of IPerge). Cf. SEG 49:1889.

47. Lucianic (L) text of Esther is contained in manuscripts 19 (Brooke–McLean: b'), 93 (e2), 108 (b), 319 (y), and part of 392. See R. Hanhart, *Esther: Vetus Testamentum graecum auctoritate Academiae Scientiarum Gottingensis editum* (Göttingen: Vandenhoeck and Ruprecht, 1966), 15–16; E. Tov, "The 'Lucianic' Text of the Canonical and the Apocryphal Sections of Esther: A Rewritten Biblical Book" (revised version), in E. Tov, *The Greek and Hebrew Bible: Collected Essays on the Septuagint* (VTSup 72; Leiden: Brill, 1999), 535–48. Note that this text is printed separately by Hanhart, but not included at all by Rahlfs.

48. For summary of the debates, see Tov, "'Lucianic' Text," 540–41.

49. C. Cavalier, *Esther* (La Bible d'Alexandrie 12; Paris: Cerfs, 2012), 115, suggests there is an eschatological tenor brought in by the use of κυρίευσις in place of the word κρίσις found in the OG version.

The noun κυρίευσις, an obvious derivation from the verb κυριεύω, does not appear in LSJ but was added by the *Supplement* (90) and *Rev.Supplement* ('gaining possession of,' 190), with a reference to *Marm.Par.* 109. One can easily see why this has not been taken up further in Septuagint lexicons;[50] not only is it hidden away in the *Rev.Supplement*, but *Marm.Par* is not included in the list of abbreviations of the *Rev.Supplement* and no date is indicated. A quotation in the context is at least given (ἀπὸ τῆς Πτολεμαίου Αἰγύπτου κυριεύσεως), which indicates we are in the Ptolemaic period. The abbreviation is not included since it is already in the main LSJ list, as *Marmor Parium* (*The Parian Marble*),[51] the title for IG XII 5.444. This particular inscription, from the island of Paros in the Cyclades, is a chronicle listing events from the second millennium B.C.E. down to 264/3 B.C.E., and is to be dated at this end point.

ἀπὸ τῆς Ἀλεξάν[δ]ρου μεταλλαγῆς καὶ Πτολεμαίου Αἰγύπτο[υ] κυριεύσεως (line 109a–b)

From the death of Alexander and Ptolemy's gaining control of Egypt

The noun appears again in later inscriptions (e.g., SEG 51:833.6; Macedonia, c. 230 C.E.), but this one is sufficient to indicate its use earlier than the translation of Esther.

16. πειρατής

A late word in Greek for 'pirate,' πειρατής, makes three appearances in the Septuagint (Hos 6:9; Job 16:9; 25:3). The Septuagint lexicons recognize its presence in Polybius (as recorded in LSJ 1355) and therefore follow their practice of marking it by "neol.?" in LEH and an asterisk in GELS. The second century B.C.E., the time of Polybius, is also the likely century for the translations of the Minor Prophets and Job. Therefore, the marking of the word as a potential neologism is once more misleading. LSJ already records one piece of epigraphic evidence (Supp.Epigr. [= SEG] 3.378 B 11) of the second or first century B.C.E., which would also place us in the same timeframe as Polybius and LXX Minor Prophets.

In the Septuagint there are some cognates of πειρατής: πειρατήριον 'gang of brigands or pirates' (LSJ 1355; Gen 49:19) and πειρατεύω 'attack, of a robber-band,' (Gen 49:19). The adjective πειρατικός 'fit for piracy' also exists in Greek. The words are most probably derivatives of πεῖρα 'trial,

---

50. It is characteristically marked by an asterisk in GELS 419.
51. F. Jacoby, *Das marmor Parium, herausgegeben und erklärt* (Berlin: Weidmann, 1904). Later republished as F. Jacoby, *Die Fragmente der griechischen Historiker*, II B (Leiden: Brill, 1997 reprint) 992–1005; *Kommentar* II B (Leiden: Brill, 1993 reprint), 665–702.

attempt.'[52] There are a good number of examples of the word πειρατής in Hellenistic inscriptions, including a dedication from Delos to Zeus and Astarte by one Damon, son of Demetrios, from Ascalon (Ἀσκαλωνίτης). He gives thanks, σωθεὶς ἀπὸ πειρατῶν "having been saved from pirates" (IDelos 2305.4; after 166 B.C.E.). The earliest instance may be IG IX 1² 1.15 (Aitolia; 300–262 B.C.E.) but the context is limited, preventing anything more being said about it. Nonetheless, IPArk 24 (SEG 25:447), a decree granting amnesty in 273 B.C.E., records the success of individuals at expelling pirates (τὸς πειρατὰς ἐξέβαλε, ll. 3, 8). From near the same time comes SEG 24:154, an Attic decree made during the Chremonidean war to honor Epichares, commander of the Attic deme Rhamnous. He had offered a deal to the pirates to buy back each captured deme member, either in the year 268/7 or slightly later in 265/4:[53]

> ἐκόλασε δὲ καὶ τοὺ|[ς κ]αθηγουμένους εἰς τ[ὴ]ν χώραν τοῖς πειραταῖς, λαβὼν καὶ ἐξετάσας αὐτούς, ὄν|[τα]ς ἐκ τῆς πόλεως, [ἀξίω]ς ὧν ἔπραττον· (ll. 21–23)

> he also punished those who had [i]ntroduced the pirates into t[h]e land, men from the city, arresting and interrogating them [in a way that was fitting] for what they did.[54]

There is sufficient attestation then in the third century B.C.E. to show that the Septuagint does not provide the first uses of the word.[55] It served as a pejorative term for raider of plunderer,[56] synonymous with λῃστής, and it would have been well established in the language by the second century for the translators to have used it without a second thought.

17. σανιδωτός

Exod 27:8 records the construction of the altar of acacia wood:

> κοῖλον σανιδωτὸν ποιήσεις αὐτό κατὰ τὸ παραδειχθέν σοι ἐν τῷ ὄρει, οὕτως ποιήσεις αὐτό.

---

52. *EDG* 2: 1162–63. There is a good discussion of the early occurrences of πειρατής in P. de Souza, *Piracy in the Graeco-Roman World* (Cambridge: Cambridge University Press, 1999), 3–9.

53. Discussion in de Souza, *Piracy*, 65–66. He gives this inscription as the earliest example of the word πειρατής (3).

54. Translation by M. M. Austin, *The Hellenistic World from Alexander to the Roman Conquest: A Selection of Ancient Sources in Translation* (2nd ed.; Cambridge: Cambridge University Press, 2006), 133–34 no. 62.

55. See too IG XII 7.386 (Amorgos, before 200 B.C.E.) and the adjective πειρατικός in SIG 454 = IG II² 1225 (shortly after 250 B.C.E.; de Souza, *Piracy*, 4–5). De Souza, *Piracy*, 5–8, discusses and dismisses some speculative suggestions for yet earlier attestations.

56. So de Souza, *Piracy*, 4.

Hollow, with planks, you shall make it. According to that which was shown to you on the mountain, so you shall make it. (NETS)

Although LSJ (1583) gives LXX Exodus as the first occurrence of σανιδωτός 'planked, boarded over,' this was updated in the *Supplement*, for the existence of the word is now clear from inventory lists from Delos.[57] In one inventory for the gymnasium in Delos, IDelos 1417 (155/4 B.C.E.; see also SEG 38:771, which dates to 156/5 B.C.E.), κλίνας σαν<ι>δωτάς 'boarded beds' (lines 50 and 55) are listed.[58] Similar uses are found from the same period in Delos in other inscriptions too.[59]

18. τίναγμα

LSJ (1795) only offers two references for the noun τίναγμα, a late Roman epigrammist Claudian, preserved in the *Anthologia Palatina* (9.139), and the Greek version of Job:

ὅτε ἐποίησεν οὕτως, ὑετὸν ἠρίθμησεν [καὶ ὁδὸν ἐν τινάγματι φωνάς] (Job 28:26)

when he had done this, he counted the rain [and a way in the shaking, sounds]

As indicated by the square brackets here, the word is to be found in the asterisked portion of Job and not the Old Greek, as might have been implied by LSJ. This means it is not part of the Old Greek, but was added by Origen and marked as originally missing from the Greek in comparison to the Hebrew. The additions by Origen are usually thought to have been from the version attributed to Theodotion in the second century C.E., although they can be more tentatively placed in a translation tradition close to *kaige*, somewhere between the Old Greek and Aquila, a development that is "at least typological if not chronological."[60]

It would seem clear that τίναγμα as a deverbal from τινάσσω must mean 'shaking.' Indeed, even if the Greek is syntactically awkward, the rendering in Job of the Hebrew for thunderbolt by 'shaking' would be understandable. This Greek word has now been found in an inscription from Egypt, an epitaph from the El Wardyān necropolis, west of Alexandria (IEgVers 64.9–12; TM 43990):

---

57. *Supplement* (132) and *Rev.Supplement* (273) record IDelos 1403 *bis* and IDelos 1417.

58. Cf. SEG 30:1811. J. Tréheux, *BCH* 112 (1988): 583–89.

59. IDelos 1403.29 and 33 (c. 165–157/6 B.C.E.; see also: SEG 37:692; SEG 39:711); IDelos 1408 face D left.col. II.1.8–9 (162/1–161/0? B.C.E.); IDelos 1412.46 (166–157/6 B.C.E.).

60. P. J. Gentry, *The Asterisked Materials in the Greek Job* (SBLSCS 38; Atlanta, GA: Scholars Press, 1995), 421.

... πατρίδα σῴζων
κάτθα[ν]ες, ἀντιπάλων ἀντίος ἱστάμενος,
καὶ δορὸ[ς] οὐκ ἤσχυνας ἀριζάλοιο τίναγμα,
ψυχὰν δὲ στρατιᾶς ἄμμιγα συγκατέθου·[61]

... In saving your country,
you di[e]d, by taking your stand against the enemies,
and you had no fear of the shaking of the glinting lan[ce],
but you breathed your last amidst your company

This epitaph in elegiac distichs is for a soldier, mourned by his fellow soldiers but considered happy for having died among companions. It is written in poetic language, combining Homeric forms with Doric and Ionic. When first published the inscription was identified as from the second century C.E.,[62] but a good case has been made that the lettering and context suggests the second or first century B.C.E.[63] This places it at a time somewhat earlier than the asterisked material in Job.

19. ὑπέρμαχος

In the Septuagint ὑπέρμαχος 'champion, defender' only appears in Wisdom (10:20; 16:17) and 2 Maccabees (8:36; 14:34). It is not attested at all in papyri, reflective of the everyday, non-military character of the papyri. It is also not attested in literature before the Septuagint, but afterwards it appears in the Sibylline Oracles, Philo, and the Church Fathers. In Wisdom the noun is naturally used metaphorically, both in apposition to God's hand (Wis 10:20, τήν τε ὑπέρμαχόν σου χεῖρα ᾔνεσαν "they praised your defending hand") and to the world as "defender of the righteous" (16:17, ὑπέρμαχος γὰρ ὁ κόσμος ἐστὶν δικαίων). Nevertheless, in 2 Macca-

---

61. This is the reading of C. Gallavotti ("Postilla alla nuova epigrafe alessandrina," in Ἀντίδωρον *Hugoni Henrico Paoli oblatum: Miscellanea philologica* [Pubblicazioni dell'Istituto di filologia classica 8; Genoa: Istituto di filologia classica, 1956], 323–24), which has been accepted by others (e.g., P. M. Fraser, "Bibliography: Graeco-Roman Egypt: Greek Inscriptions (1956)," *JEA* 43 (1957): 101–9 [102–3]). The original publication by A. Traversa reads τιν ἄγμα, taking τίν as Doric for σοί (Pindar, *Isthm.* 6.5) ("L'iscrizione metrica per Felice," in Ἀντίδωρον *Hugoni Henrico Paoli oblatum*, 283–322). Traversa tried to justify his readings again ("Replica a una 'postilla,'" *Epigraphica* 17 [1955]: 15–32), but with little success, as observed by P. M. Fraser, "Bibliography: Graeco-Roman Egypt: Greek Inscriptions (1957)," *JEA* 44 (1958): 108–16 (110). Further improvements on the readings appear in C. Gallavotti, "La Stele di Ammonio," *La Parola del Passato* 12 (1957): 375–77.

62. A. Traversa, "Iscrizione metrica da Alessandria," *Aegyptus* 35 (1955): 137–38 (138); A. Traversa, "L'iscrizione metrica per Felice," 284–85; P. M. Fraser, "Bibliography: Graeco-Roman Egypt: Greek Inscriptions (1956)," 102. Cf. SEG 15:853.

63. C. Gallavotti, "Postilla alla nuova epigrafe alessandrina," 324; E. Bernand, *Inscriptions métriques de l'Égypte gréco-romaine: recherches sur la poésie épigrammatique des grecs en Égypte* (Annales littéraires de l'Université de Besançon 98; Paris: Belles lettres, 1969), 260.

bees as well ὑπέρμαχος is applied to God as defender of his people (2 Macc 8:36: κατήγγελλεν ὑπέρμαχον ἔχειν τοὺς Ιουδαίους "they proclaimed that the Jews had a defender"; 14:34: ἐπεκαλοῦντο τὸν διὰ παντὸς ὑπέρμαχον τοῦ ἔθνους ἡμῶν "they called upon the perpetual defender of our nation").

The cognate verb ὑπερμαχέω does appear in classical literature but rarely, and therefore it is a puzzle to find these uses in the Septuagint. The solution is to be sought in the inscriptions, where the verb occasionally appears (IG XII 6.1.7.17; Samos, 5 B.C.E.) but the noun is marginally more frequent. Excluding later Roman examples, when it becomes an ecclesiastical title (IGLSyria 3.1.9119), instances appear in Crete, Delos, and Lydia. The first two of these locations were under Ptolemaic rule, but Lydia was under the Seleucids followed by the Attalids, indicating a broad distribution of this title. It is always paired with other titles: in a Doric inscription from Crete [β]ο[α]|θὸς καὶ ὑπερμάχος τᾶς ἁμᾶς πόλεος "helper and defender of the same city" (IKret I xix 3.28–29, end of second century B.C.E.);[64] and in Delos Λόχου το[ῦ] Κα<λ>[λιμήδου] | [τ]οῦ συγγενοῦς καὶ ὑπερμάχου | καὶ ὑπομνηματογράφου καὶ στρατηγοῦ "of Lochos son of Kal[limedes, t]he kinsman and defender and recorder and general".[65] In Lydia the *strategos* Mogetes is honored in an epitaph, having gained glory through death in combat (second century B.C.E.):

μούνα καὶ πρόκριτον πάτρας καὶ ὑπέρμαχον ἀε[ὶ]
Ῥώμας κυδίστοις θήκατ᾽ ἐν ἀγεμόσι. (TAM V 1 468b.13–14 [SEG 28:891])

She (Athena) alone placed you, the chosen one and continua[l] defender of the fatherland, among the most glorious of Rome's generals.

It thus seems that ὑπέρμαχος 'champion, defender,' though hardly attested in extant sources, was used in a broad geographical area under the Hellenistic monarchies. It was one of a series of titles used for officials, presumably, by its appearance only in lists, one of lesser importance than other titles and therefore not used frequently. The adoption of such a term for God in the Septuagint is comparable to the adoption in the Septuagint of terms used of the Ptolemaic king in papyri, including ἀντιλήπωρ and βοηθός, the latter paired with ὑπέρμαχος in some inscriptions.[66]

---

64. A. Chaniotis, *Die Verträge zwischen kretischen Poleis in der hellenistischen Zeit* (Stuttgart: Steiner, 1996), 73a.

65. *ABSA* 56 (1961): 29, 76. See the similar wording in *ABSA* 56 (1961): 28, 75.

66. See in particular O. Montevecchi, "Quaedam de graecitate psalmorum cum papyris comparata," in *Bibbia e papiri. Luce dai papiri sulla Bibbia greca, a cura di A. Passoni*

20. φύλαγμα

The word φύλαγμα has been known from sources much later than the time of the Septuagint. However, the word can now be identified in a contemporary inscription. As a derivative of the verb, it is not unexpected that such a form is attested.

As the word is always found in the Septuagint (eight times) in the set phrase to represent the Hebrew *figura etymologica* on the verb שׁמר, φύλαγμα might appear to be a Septuagint invention. Thus:

וּשְׁמַרְתֶּם אֶת־מִשְׁמֶרֶת יְהוָה

φυλάξεσθε τὰ φυλάγματα κυρίου (Lev 8:35)

The noun מִשְׁמֶרֶת can often mean 'watch, observation' (e.g., Exod 12:6), but in the cases where it is translated by φύλαγμα it always denotes the obligations or precepts of the Lord. The derivation of the noun from the verb is standard, and the translators appear to have focused more on the form than on the sense in context. Even though from the viewpoint of translation technique the translators were concerned about the form, it is still informative from a lexicological perspective. Apart from biblical and related literature, the word only appears in literature in grammatical discussions (Aelius Herodian) describing the morphology. Nevertheless, it is attested in one early inscription from Nicomedia:[67]

... ἄμπαυμα μόχθων καὶ φύλαγμα σωμ[άτων]
ἔθεντο κοινὸν ἐς τὸ τοῦ βίου [τέλος] (TAM IV 1 303)

They built this as a joint resting-place from their toils and a protection for their bod[ies] for the [end] of their life

TAM IV 1 303 is an inscription on a chalk sarcophagus referring to the sarcophagus as a φύλαγμα for the bodies. It seems clear that ἄμπαυμα (variant for ἀνάπαυμα) is in parallelism with φύλαγμα and so denotes the tomb itself, but we should not follow Jones in thinking both words have a similar connotation. He renders φύλαγμα as 'receptacle,'[68] implying it denotes an object that contains the bodies in a similar fashion to ἄμπαυμα. Given the noun's derivation from the verb, it would be better to define it as an item that offers protection, a 'defense' or 'protection.' There may be some poetic irony that the sarcophagus provides a resting place for a dead body

Dell'Acqua (Estudios de Papirologia y Filologia Biblica 5; Barcelona: Institut de Teologia fondamental, Seminari de papirologia, 1999), 97–120.

67. S. Şahin, "Neue Inschriften von der bithynischen Halbinsel," *ZPE* 18 (1975): 27–48 (42 no. 125).

68. C. P. Jones, "Two Epigrams from Nicomedia and Its Region," *ZPE* 21 (1976): 189–91 (189).

and a protection for mere bones, although the idea of protection for a grave recalls the frequent request in curse inscriptions on tombs not to disturb the bones. This inscription, therefore, confirms the existence of the noun φύλαγμα in extrabiblical Greek. It remains possible that both the composer of the sarcophagus inscription and the Septuagint translators independently invented the noun as a derivation of the verb, in the former case as a noun that is morphologically parallel to ἄμπαυμα, and in the latter as a cognate accusative phrase. Nevertheless, the meaning 'defense' or 'protection' in the Septuagint is appropriate within the limits of the translation technique.

CHAPTER 5

Semantics, Grammar, and Register

Debates over the nature of biblical Greek have often centered on the extent to which words are given new meanings or used in syntactically unexpected phrases. For the Septuagint, oddities can sometimes be attributed to the translation technique and the interference of the source language. At times such conclusions require modification, when equivalent semantic or syntactic forms are found in documentary evidence. Our fragmentary sources only provide a snapshot in time of the language, but this means that any comparable example is of value. Such examples do not rule out the Septuagint being odd, especially in the frequency of particular uses, but indicate that the translators were working within the standards of language and were adapting uses from daily language.

Related to semantics is the register of words and the connotations conveyed. There will always be an element of subjectivity in deciding on register, but the inscriptions provide additional and at times contrasting evidence to papyri in this. This chapter is divided into three parts, although there is a degree of artificiality in the distinctions: semantics, grammar, and register.

1. Semantics

1.a. ἀγαπάω and ἠγαπημένος

Much has been written on the meaning of ἀγάπη and the verb ἀγαπάω, and the extent to which one can impute a theological significance to the word group. It is disputed whether they were deliberately chosen in certain contexts in differentiation from other words from the field of 'love.'[1] Recourse to inscriptions will not solve that knotty debate, which is largely built upon questionable semantic methods. However, given the increase in

---

1. J. Barr, "Words for Love in Biblical Greek," in *The Glory of Christ in the New Testament: Studies in Christology in Memory of George Bradford Caird* (ed. L. D. Hurst and N. T. Wright; Oxford: Clarendon, 1987), 3–18. Cf. S. E. Porter, *Studies in the Greek New Testament: Theory and Practice* (New York: Peter Lang, 1996), 61–62; D. A. Carson, *Exegetical Fallacies* (2nd ed.; Grand Rapids, MI: Baker, 1996), 53, 60.

use in ἀγάπη and cognates in the Septuagint compared to classical Greek some attention to the use in Koine can be informative. It has been shown from both documentary and literary evidence that ἀγαπάω gradually came to supplant φιλέω as the word of choice for Greek speakers. Therefore, the Septuagint preference for ἀγαπάω was motivated by its usage in contemporary language.

Although the words are rare in inscriptions, epigraphic evidence demonstrates the wide geographical spread of the words. While found in Egyptian inscriptions, the verb is also attested as far away as Kandahar:[2]

ἔδει ... διδάσκαλον καὶ πατέρα καὶ μητέρα | ἐπαισχύνεσθαι καὶ θαυμάζειν, φίλους καὶ ἑταίρους ἀγαπᾶν (IGExtrEast 292.8–9)

They ought to be modest towards and revere their teacher, mother, and father, and to love friends and companions

Particularly informative is the use of the perfect passive participle, ἠγαπημένος. The form is frequent in the Septuagint, used of both Israel and individuals:

παῖς μου Ιακωβ καὶ ὁ ἠγαπημένος Ισραηλ, ὃν ἐξελεξάμην· (Isa 44:2)

my son Jacob and the beloved Israel, whom I have chosen

ἠγαπημένον ὑπὸ θεοῦ καὶ ἀνθρώπων Μωυσῆν, οὗ τὸ μνημόσυνον ἐν εὐλογίαις (Sir 45:1)

beloved by God and humans was Moses, whose memory is for a blessing

In papyri there is only one highly damaged example of ἠγαπημένος before the Roman period:

[Πτολεμαῖ]ος αἰωνόβιος, ἠγαπ[ημένος ὑπὸ τῆς Ἴσιδος] (P.Münch. 3.1.45.12 [TM 5248]; 221–205 B.C.E.)

Immortal [Ptolem]y, bel[oved by Isis]

Such expressions are more frequent and better represented in inscriptions, as for example the designation of Ptolemy in the Rosetta stone (196 B.C.E.), where he is referred to a number of times as ἠγαπημένος ὑπὸ τοῦ Φθᾶ (OGIS 90.4, 8, 9, 37, 49 [TM 8809]). It appears to be an expression of special favor towards an individual, and the Septuagint participates in the politico-theological language of the Hellenistic monarchs.

---

2. This example is used by J. A. L. Lee, "The Vocabulary of the Septuagint and Documentary Evidence," in *Handbuch zur Septuaginta: IV Sprache* (ed. E. Bons and J. Joosten; Gütersloh: Gütersloher Verlagshaus), forthcoming. I am grateful to him for supplying me with an advanced copy of this entry.

1.b. ἀδελφότης, ὁμόνοια, and φιλοπολίτης

Given the official nature of many inscriptions, epigraphic evidence reflects political language better than the papyri. A number of words associated with political agreements or propaganda are to be found that illustrate examples in the Septuagint. In 1 Maccabees the Hasmoneans renew relations with the Spartans on the basis of a long-standing ἀδελφότης 'brotherhood' (1 Macc 12:10, 17), which 4 Maccabees extends to a bond between martyrs (4 Macc 9:23; 10:3, 15; 13:19, 27; cf. 1 Pet 2:17; 5:9). In LSJ (21) the references for ἀδελφότης are from the Roman period (e.g., Vettius Valens 2.28, second century C.E.), but its earliest use can be traced back to just before the time of 1 Maccabees at some point in the second century B.C.E. An inscription from Aphrodisias (IAph2007 8.210.9)[3] is a dedication to Zeus Philios, Homonoia, and Thea Rome, by the people (οἱ δῆμοι) of Aphrodisias, Kibyra, and Tabai, on the occasion of the swearing of an alliance:

> . . . ποιησάμενοι καὶ ὅρκι[α]
> καθ᾽ ἱερῶν νεοκαύτων καὶ σφ[ά]-
> [για] ὑπὲρ τῆς πρὸς ἀ<λλ>ήλους φ[ύσ]-
> [ει] συμμαχίας καὶ ὁμονοίας
> [αἰ]ωνίου καὶ ἀδελφότητος

who have taken oath[s] over newly burnt offerings and made blood-[offerings] for their n[atural] alliance, [et]ernal concord, and brotherhood with each other[4]

The letter forms can be located probably in the second century B.C.E., and some have dated the inscription to shortly after 167 B.C.E., when Rome granted Caria its freedom (Polybius, *Hist.* 21.24.7; 30.5.12).[5] The simplicity and lack of sophistication of the language reflecting a chancery style could imply too the early days of the city before the citizens had developed experience of diplomacy. The expression used here is precisely that in 1 Maccabees, invoking blood relations that are alleged to have existed between the cities.

In the same inscription we find a very rare personification of ὁμόνοια 'concord' as the harmony between cities (cf. IG II² 687.31, 34), known much more from coin inscriptions. The noun more commonly refers to

---

3. PHI Aphrodisias 197; J. M. Reynolds, *Aphrodisias and Rome: Documents from the Excavation of the Theatre at Aphrodisias Conducted by Kenan T. Erim, Together with Some Related Texts* (Journal of Roman Studies Monograph 1; London: Society for the Promotion of Roman Studies, 1982), no. 1.

4. Translation from Reynolds, *Aphrodisias and Rome*, 7.

5. Reynolds, *Aphrodisias and Rome*, 6–7.

civil peace among a group, and this is how it is used within the Septuagint (Pss 54:15; 82:6; Wis 10:5; 18:9; Sir 25:1; cf. 4 Macc 3:21; 13:25). Inscriptions frequently speak of enhancing the ὁμόνοια of groups, such as all the Athenians (πάντων Ἀθηναίων, SEG 25:112.16; 196/5 B.C.E.).

A final example is the term φιλοπολίτης 'loyal citizen' (2 Macc 14:37), used as a positive term in 2 Maccabees to describe one loyal to Judaism and his fellow people and observant of the law. LEH (648) marks it as a neologism, as it is only found in Plutarch and Dio Chrysostom among literature of the time period. It seems unlikely that the author of 2 Maccabees has invented the word and it is attested in at least one inscription (IEph 1390.3) from the Hellenistic period:

[καθὼς δί]κα[ιόν] τε καὶ [ἐ]πιβάλ[λ]ον ἐστὶν ἀνδρὶ φιλοπολίτηι καὶ φροντίζοντι δόξης καὶ τῆς παρὰ τοῖς πολίταις [εὐφη]||[μίας·

[as it is] both [ri]gh[t] and [fi]tti[n]g for a person who is concerned for his fellow citizens and mindful of honor and the [good reputation] of the citizens

It is also once found as an epithet of Tiberius Claudius (SEG 31:913.3) in first-century Aphrodisias (41–54 C.E.). It is illustrative of the political use from which the authors drew and the likelihood that such terms were more common than the scarcity in our sources would suggest.

1.c. ἀρχιμάγειρος

The title ἀρχιμάγειρος is frequent in the Septuagint to denote a class of official. It renders either רב־טבחים (Aramaic רב־טבחיא) or שר־טבחים, and it can easily be seen why some might see it as a stereotyped rendering.[6] The Hebrew and Aramaic terms, although apparently denoting official titles in Egypt (such as that of Potiphar in the Joseph saga),[7] derive from the verb 'to bake' and therefore the Greek would seem to be a standard equivalent derived from the verb μαγειρεύω, 'to be a cook, cook meat' (LSJ 1071). Nevertheless, the Hebrew idea of baking also has the connotation of killing, and hence at first sight the Hebrew seems to have a fuller and more specified sense than the Greek. Hiebert, discounting the evidence of Plutarch (late first century C.E.) as too late,[8] accepts that the Greek noun does not have a "metaphorical" extension in the way the Hebrew and Aramaic

---

6. E.g, R. J. V. Hiebert, "Lexicography and the Translation of a Translation: The NETS Version and the Septuagint of Genesis," *BIOSCS* 37 (2004): 73–86 (75–77). One might note its occurrences in Philo and Josephus, all of which are in discussions of the biblical passages and therefore not independent evidence.

7. Hiebert notes the translation of Josephus.

8. By his own admission, Hiebert is dependent on LSJ.

do, and concludes that the Septuagint produces a stereotypical rendering that creates semantic dissonance between the Hebrew and the Greek.[9] The lexicons provide brief glosses for the noun, naturally not entering into discussion of the extended or metaphorical sense. LSJ recognizes the basic meaning of 'chief cook' (253), citing LXX Genesis and Philo, but also records that it is a "title of a great officer in Oriental courts," and (as ἀρχιμαγειρεύς) a "dignitary in Mithraic cult." GELS likewise opts for the straightforward rendering 'chief cook' (95), while LEH (86), perhaps under the influence of the context and the Hebrew/Aramaic equivalents, chooses 'chief of a royal guard, *lit.* chief cook', noting it as a neologism.

Inscriptions provide important evidence and supplement that of LSJ. Of three inscriptions containing the noun, the oldest from Olympia (IOlympia 62.17) is (late) first-century B.C.E., and very close to the likely time of the translation of Greek Daniel. The Greek inscription from Olympia is a list of names with titles, some reflecting a high social status but some less significant. We cannot conclude from this the social status of an ἀρχιμάγειρος, but we can infer that the term was seen as an official title and not a mere occupation.[10] The two other inscriptions are from the later Roman period, with the spelling ἀρχιμαγειρεύς (IG X 2.1.65 from the third century C.E. and SEG 51:886 from the second or third century C.E.) and seem to refer to members of cult associations.

Corroboration might be sought from an occurrence of the noun in Aelius Herodian where, in an explanation of the formation of ἀρχι- prefix nouns, he cites for illustration: ἀρχιστράτηγος· ἀρχισατράπης· ἀρχιμάγειρος. The other two are both military officials and this adds to the impression of a more dignified position than that of a cook. The evidence does at the least indicate that the title was not so unknown that it could not be used for illustration.[11] In the Septuagint the ἀρχιμάγειρος is an official in the Pharaonic and Persian courts, and the epigraphic evidence confirms the use of the word as an official title.

1.d. διασάφησις

Although διασάφησις (Gen 40:8; 2 Esd 5:6; 7:11) makes its only appearance in the Septuagint among extant literature, it seems to have a dif-

---

9. Hiebert, "Lexicography," 76–77.

10. M. Donderer, *Die Architekten der späten römischen Republik und der Kaiserzeit: Epigraphische Zeugnisse* (Erlanger Forschungen A: Geisteswissenschaften 69; Erlangen: Universitätsbibliothek Erlangen-Nürnberg, 1996), A69.

11. The word continues as a Latin loanword *archimagirus*. It appears in two Latin epitaphs (*AE* 1973, 0084 and *AE* 1937, 0159) referring to freedmen by the title, and in one case (*AE* 1937, 0159) his role as a cook is noted. In Juvenal (*Satire 9*) too *archimagirus* refers to the workers in the house amongst whom one would rather not be a source of gossip.

ferent sense in the two Septuagint books. In Gen 40:8 διασάφησις refers to Joseph's interpretation of a dream used in close association with the verb συγκρίνω 'to decree' (Gen 40:8) and its cognate noun σύγκρισις (Gen 40:12):

εἶπεν δὲ αὐτοῖς Ιωσηφ Οὐχὶ διὰ τοῦ θεοῦ ἡ διασάφησις αὐτῶν ἐστιν;

And Joseph said to them, "Is it not by God that their interpretation comes?"

The meaning here is not in dispute. The context of Joseph's dreams requires the sense 'interpretation,' and the verb from which the noun derives, διασαφέω, means in classical Greek 'make quite clear, show plainly' (LSJ 411; i.e., 'to interpret'; Aristotle, *de spiritu* 482a; cf. *Aristeas* 38). The problem arises when we consider the occurrences in 2 Esdras:

διασάφησις ἐπιστολῆς, ἧς ἀπέστειλεν Θανθαναι ὁ ἔπαρχος (2 Esd 5:6)

The *diasafēsis* of the letter that Thanthanai the *eparch* sent

καὶ αὕτη ἡ διασάφησις τοῦ διατάγματος, οὗ ἔδωκεν Αρθασασθα τῷ Εσδρα (2 Esd 7:11)

And this is the *diasafēsis* of the decree, which Arthasastha gave to Ezra

The presumed Aramaic *Vorlage* has the noun פרשגן 'copy,' which in 1 Esd 6:6 has been accurately rendered by the Greek ἀντίγραφον. The standard classical lexicons follow LSJ, which does not refer to the 2 Esdras examples: "explanation, interpretation, LXX Ge.40.8" (cf. DGE 1030: "interpretación, aclaración (de los sueños)"; and, Montanari 516: "spiegazione, interpretazione VT. Gen 40.8 (di sogni)"). Faced with the problem of accounting for 2 Esdras, the Septuagint lexicons, although aware of a cognate verb, are primarily guided by context in offering definitions for the noun, even if they indicate the tentative nature of the definitions. LEH (145: "explanation, interpretation; copy?, translation?; neol.") offer interpretations based on the context. GELS (120) tries to show the semantic connection between the two uses ("1. act of explaining; 2. text publicly made known"), recognizing that the noun in 2 Esdras denotes a decree but wishing to show its inherent relationship to the verb 'to make clear.'

The solution might be simpler than the lexicons make out. One possibility that should be noted is that in 2 Esdras there might be a translation error. The translator might have misunderstood the Aramaic פרשגן 'copy' as a derivative of the verb פרש 'to interpret.' He would then have provided a translation denoting 'interpretation,' especially as elsewhere in the Joseph tale interpretation is denoted in Hebrew by פרש. However, documentary evidence offers an alternative explanation. In Koine papyri the verb has a specialized administrative sense of 'giving information' (usually to a superior: e.g., BGU 6.1211), although only the verb, and never the noun, appears in papyri. As a result we might well follow others and call the noun a "Jewish coinage," even if as a derivative of this specialized administrative sense.[12] Caution should nonetheless be exercised, and Lee indeed had astutely observed some time ago that it is, "probably accidental that it has not turned up elsewhere ... Any Greek speaker who needed a noun from the verb διασαφέω would be likely to have employed διασάφησις."[13] As it happens, two possible examples of the noun have appeared, even if they are both found in highly damaged contexts. The existence of the cognate verb and the contexts of the inscriptions justify in each case the reconstructions by the editors. The first is from Mysia in Thessaly (IG IX 2):[14]

Π.ΑΝ [ἡ δια]σάφησις.[— — — — — —]
[βασ]ιλέως Γ. . . .A.A[— — — — — —] (lines 7–8)

The inscription is dated to the first century B.C.E., precisely within our time period, and, assuming the reconstruction is correct, confirms the existence of the noun in extrabiblical Greek. The context is clearly that of a public decree (relating to a conflict between Gonnoi and Herakleion) and therefore comparable to the context in 2 Esdras. The second occurrence, from the turn of the era (c. 15 B.C.E. to 15 C.E.), is a long honorary decree from Cyzicus in Anatolia and is well preserved, except for the very opening:[15]

καὶ τοὺς ἄ[λλου]ς [π]ο[λίτας] - - -
αὐτῶν ἐπὶ [διας]άφης[ιν - -]ΥΔΙ - - -
κήρυκ[ος - -] δημος[ίᾳ?] τὸ πρᾶ[γμα? - - - Δη]-
μήτ[ρ]ιον Οἰνιάδ[ου] ἀρ[ετῆς ἕ]ν[εκεν καὶ εὐνοίας] - - -

and the re[st of the cit]iz[ens
their on the [de]cree
of a hera[ld   ] in pub[lic] the a[ct   De]
met[r]ius son of Oinia[s] for his exce[llence and favour]

---

12. So G. Zuntz, "Aristeas Studies II: Aristeas on the translation of the Torah," *JSS* 4 (1959): 109–26 (112).

13. Lee, *Lexical Study*, 47.

14. B. Helly, *Gonnoi* (2 vols.; Amsterdam: Hakkert, 1973), 2: no. 104.

15. Published in R. Cagnat et al., *Inscriptiones Graecae ad res Romanas pertinentes*, IV (Paris: Leroux, 1927), 159. See too SEG 55:1329. Republished by É. Chiricat, "Funérailles publiques et enterrement au gymnase à l'époque hellénistique," in *Citoyenneté et participation à la basse époque hellénistique* (ed. P. Fröhlich and C. Müller; Hautes Etudes du monde gréco-romain 35; Geneva: Droz, 2005), 214–22 (207–23).

It is in the opening that the editor has reconstructed the reading ἐπὶ [διας]άφης[ιν. While this evidence is fragmentary and has to be used with caution, these inscriptions, both being public decrees, support the meaning in 2 Esdras of a copy of a decree and at least confirm that it is not a mistranslation of the Hebrew.

1.e. εὐλογέω

A well-known equivalent in the Septuagint is the verb εὐλογέω and its cognates. It continues the meaning from classical Greek of 'to give thanks' or 'praise' (Aristophanes, *Eccl.* 454), and its use in praising a deity is not unknown either (Euripides, *Suppl.* 927).[16] What is distinctive about the Septuagint use is both its frequency and its apparent extension of meaning in the sense of 'to bless,' especially of God blessing humans. The verb εὐλογέω and its cognate noun εὐλογία have often been taken to be Semitisms.[17] Its use has arisen from lexical stereotyping, where the Hebrew ברך was translated by εὐλογέω both when it denoted 'to praise' and when it denoted 'to bless.'

At first sight the inscriptional evidence of the use of the verb εὐλογέω and the noun εὐλογία seems too distant for its relevance to the Septuagint. They appear in confessions from northeast Lydia and Sardis of the early Roman period (e.g., SEG 38:1234). Pleket, however, has argued that these represent a longer tradition of praise of deities, and by this stage reflect an institutionalization of this sort of divine praise.[18] In these Lydian inscriptions the principal god praised is Men. In Egypt we find the best examples, if fewer than the Lydian inscriptions. In El Armana there is the ambiguous graffito εὐλογῶ τὸν [θεόν] (SB 1:3692 [TM 98376]), while in Antinooupolis a Greek who identifies himself as Thracian (Θρᾶιξ) praises both Pan, the god who follows the right path, εὐλογ[ῶ] τὸν Εὔο[δο]ν θεόν (SB 5:8562 [TM 47435], l. 3), and Isis, εὐλογῶ τὴν Εἶσιν (SB 5:8563 [TM 99205], 3). It seems likely that the terms form part of Greek religious language and therefore are presumably an autonomous development in Greek, rather than arising from Jewish influence.

---

16. For a full discussion of the verb in classical and Septuagint uses, see recently J. Joosten, "Le vocabulaire de la Septante et la question du sociolecte des juifs alexandrins: Le cas du verbe εὐλογέω, «bénir»," in *Septuagint Vocabulary: Pre-History, Usage, Reception* (ed. E. Bons and J. Joosten; SBLSCS 58; Atlanta, GA: SBL, 2011), 13–23; J. Joosten, "The Historical and Theological Lexicon of the Septuagint: A Sample Entry—εὐλογέω," in *XIV Congress of the IOSCS, Helsinki, 2010* (ed. M. K. H. Peters; SBLSCS, 59; Atlanta, GA: SBL, 2013), 347–55.

17. Cf. NETS: 3 ("calque").

18. H. W. Pleket, "Religious History as the History of Mentality: The 'Believer' as Servant of the Deity in the Greek World," in *Faith, Hope and Worship: Aspects of Religious Mentality in the Ancient World* (ed. H. S. Versnel; Leiden: Brill, 1981), 152–92.

Pleket has suggested naturally that the authors of the inscriptions and the Septuagint translators chose a more solemn word than the secularized ἔπαινος and cognates. This is not the full picture since εὐλογέω is collocated with (ἐπ)αινέω and ὑμνέω at times in the Septuagint (1 Par [=1 Chr] 16:36; 1 Esd 5:57; Pss 33[34]:2; 144[145]:1, etc.).[19] Nevertheless, the popularity of εὐλογέω over all other choices is noticeable. Pleket concludes that the seeds already sown in pagan soil, admittedly occasionally and in circumstances of private religiosity, have come to full blossom in cults that are celebrated in honor of "strongly vertical, Oriental gods."[20] Thus εὐλογέω is used of such gods as Isis, Men, and Sarapis as well as the Jewish god, reflecting similar conceptions and the adoption of similar titles.[21] If Pleket is correct, there existed a shared usage of Greek language that included the avoidance of terms used of the Greek pantheon and a focus on lesser used terms.

1.f. ὀνοματογραφία

The compound noun ὀνοματογραφία is twice found in 1 Esdras (6:11; 8:48) before appearing in Sextus Empiricus and a few later writers. The formation of the noun is standard, and the suffix -ία can indicate motion or action. Accordingly, LSJ (1233) renders the noun 'writing of names,' Montanari (1397) 'lo scrivere un nome,' and GELS (499) 'act of writing names.' This is the clear sense in Sextus Empiricus (*Against the mathematicians* 11.67):

ὥσπερ οὖν ἐν ταῖς ὀνοματογραφίαις ἄλλοτ' ἄλλα προτάττομεν στοιχεῖα, πρὸς τὰς διαφόρους περιστάσεις ἀρτιζόμενοι, καὶ τὸ μὲν δέλτα, ὅτε τὸ τοῦ Δίωνος ὄνομα γράφομεν, τὸ δὲ ἰῶτα, ὅτε τὸ τοῦ Ἴωνος ...

As then in the writings of names, we vary as to which letters we place first, guided by the different contexts, for example the *delta* when we write the name Dio, but the *iota* when we write the name Io ...

However, LEH provide a different definition, 'list of names' (LEH 440), denoting the final object, rather than the act of its production. The problem lies in the ambiguity of the two contexts in 1 Esdras. In 1 Esd 6:11 ὀνοματογραφία refers to a request for the writing down of names, but it could either denote specifically that act or the final product of the list of names:

---

19. Joosten, "Historical and Theological Lexicon," 349.

20. Pleket, "Religious History," 161.

21. G. van den Heever, "Redescribing Graeco-Roman Antiquity: On Religion and History of Religion," *Religion and Theology* 12 (2005): 211–38 (214).

ἐπηρωτήσαμεν οὖν αὐτοὺς εἵνεκεν τοῦ γνωρίσαι σοι καὶ γράψαι σοι τοὺς ἀνθρώπους τοὺς ἀφηγουμένους καὶ τὴν ὀνοματογραφίαν ἠτοῦμεν αὐτοὺς τῶν προκαθηγουμένων.

So, in order that we might inform you and write you about who the individuals are that lead them, we questioned them and asked them for the list of names of the proponents. (NETS)

Talshir sees the word as an example of the official administrative terminology in the book, but is unable to provide confirmatory examples in this case.[22] The second instance (1 Esd 8:48) is a summary of a preceding list, suggesting that it more likely denotes a list of names: πάντων ἐσημάνθη ἡ ὀνοματογραφία "the name-list of all of them was indicated." An overlooked inscription cannot resolve this ambiguity, but it can throw light on the possible meanings of the noun. The noun appears at the start of a Thracian inscription:

ὀνοματογραφία νε[ωκό]|ρων τοῦ σωτῆρος Ἀσκληπ[ιοῦ], | οἷς ἐδωρήσατο κτῆμα ἐν κ[ώ]|μῃ Σπινοπαροις (IGBulg IV 2192.2–5)

A list of ne[ophy]tes of savior Asclepi[us] to whom he gave a possession in the vil[la]ge of Spinoparis

This opening is followed by a list of names, indicating ὀνοματογραφία is self-referential to the inscribed names. The inscription has not been dated, but most of the inscriptions in the same collection derive from the first to third centuries c.e., and Mainardi draws comparison with the cult of Athena Soteira founded in the first century b.c.e.[23] The presence of Roman names favors the early centuries c.e. It therefore confirms that 'list of names' is one possible meaning for the noun, and that LEH's definition, although probably derived from contextual evidence alone, has extrabiblical support.

1.g. ὀνοκένταυρος and καμηλοπάρδαλις

You may never have encountered an onocentaur. This is unsurprising when outside the pages of the Septuagint this half-man half-donkey, the ὀνοκένταυρος, is rarely met:

---

22. Z. Talshir, *I Esdras: From Origin to Translation* (SBLSCS 47; Atlanta, GA: Society of Biblical Literature, 1999), 257.

23. M. Mainardi, "Il culto di Atena a Mesambria Pontica," in *Culti e miti greci in aree periferiche* (ed. T. Alfieri Tonini, G. Bagnasco Gianni, and F. Cordano; Aristonothos, Scritti per il Mediterraneo antico 6; Trento: Tangram Edizioni Scientifiche, 2012), 177–204.

καὶ κατοικήσουσιν ἐν αὐτῇ ὄρνεα καὶ ἐχῖνοι καὶ ἴβεις καὶ κόρακες, καὶ ἐπιβληθήσεται ἐπ' αὐτὴν σπαρτίον γεωμετρίας ἐρήμου, καὶ ὀνοκένταυροι οἰκήσουσιν ἐν αὐτῇ. (Isa 34:11)

But birds and hedgehogs and ibises and ravens shall live in it. A measuring line of desolation shall be cast over it, and donkey–centaurs shall dwell in it. (NETS)

Indeed, in contrast to the Septuagint's masculine form, LSJ (1232) gives only one other occurrence in the feminine (ἡ ὀνοκενταύρα), and this is in Aelian from the early third century C.E. Perhaps unjustifiably, LSJ separates the two occurrences into two kinds of animals. They opt for the definition of 'a kind of tailless ape' that does not do justice to the long paragraph in Aelian (*NA* 17.9). In contrast, the Septuagint (Isa 13:22; 34:11, 14) occurrences are interpreted as 'a kind of demon haunting wild places.' In reality, it is but one of a number of animals in Isaiah to be found roaming the wilderness, translating both אִיִּים (Isa 13:22; 34:14a) and לִילִית (Isa 34:14b). The association with demons is only explicit in Isa 34:14 (in Greek) where they converse with them. Even if it is a demon in this passage, demons are portrayed as types of animals, just as in Isaiah the onocentaur is named among a number of animals. It is therefore fair to ask what type of animal it is.

Aelian attributes his account of the creature to a description by one Pythagoras in the time of Ptolemy II according to the testimony of Crates of Pergamum (second century B.C.E.). The account seems somewhat fabulous, and the authenticity of the citation of Pythagoras cannot be proven. Nevertheless, the word is to be found in Italy in the Nile mosaic of Praeneste (Palestrina) from the second century B.C.E. This highly decorative mosaic is divided into two parts, the upper half depicting a sandy and rocky wasteland that represents Nubia, and the lower half depicting luscious inhabited regions that represent the Nile valley.[24] In the upper half many African animals roam, including one animal atop a rock, whose antelope-like body is joined to a human head with long flowing hair. It is labelled as ἡ ὀνοκενταύρα. Aelian had recorded that Pythagoras had considered the animal to be Ethiopian, and this would match with the mosaic's placement of it in Nubia.[25] It can be concluded therefore that the Septuagint of Isaiah is representing the Nubian wilderness and includes

---

24. The most recent detailed discussion of the mosaic is P. G. P. Meyboom, *The Nile Mosaic of Palestrina: Early Evidence of Egyptian Religion in Italy* (Leiden: Brill, 1995). See too J. F. Moffitt, "The Palestrina Mosaic with a 'Nile Scene': Philostratus and Ekphrasis; Ptolemy and Chorographia," *Zeitschrift für Kunstgeschichte* 60 (1997): 227–47.

25. Cf. Meyboom, *Nile Mosaic*, 21. For traditions on the onocentaur, see pp. 111–14.

the mythical onocentaur as one of the wild animals in that region. The Egyptian element is conveyed in Isaiah through the pairing of it with the ibis (Isa 34:11), and the hedgehog in the same passage might also be an attempt to depict this arid region.[26] The dating of the Praeneste Nile mosaic has been subject to various interpretations, but it seems likely that it can be placed in the second century, close to the time of the translation of Isaiah.[27] Variation in proposals for a date is due to the lack of strong parallels to such scenes and to the inconclusive nature of the Greek lettering. Even in the Packhum database two quite different dates are offered. For the first publication of the mosaic inscriptions in IG XIV 1302, Packhum places the mosaic in the reign of Hadrian, while for the publication in SEG 45:1452 the second century B.C.E. is offered. Dates such as the time of Sulla, Augustus, or Hadrian have been proposed as eras when Roman interest in Egypt would have been piqued, but none are definitive. The most secure dating is that of the later second century B.C.E. (c. 120–110 B.C.E.) as it is based on comparative artistic style to the Casa de Fauno in Pompeii.[28]

The Praeneste mosaic also includes the καμηλοπάρδαλις 'giraffe' (lit. 'spotted- or leopard-camel') among the animals of the Nubian desert.[29] The first occurrence of this name in Greek would appear to be in the Septuagint (Deut 14:5), taking LXX Deuteronomy as third century B.C.E. The earliest literary reference according to LSJ (872) is in the geographer Agatharchides of the second century B.C.E. (*On the Erythrean Sea* 72), although Aristophanes of Byzantium, a grammarian, might be slightly older (*History of Animals* 2.270, 278). Nevertheless, the earliest example is once more epigraphic, found in Tomb 1 of the Eastern Necropolis of Maresha (Idumea, Palestine). Taking into account the tomb layout, the loculi, the murals, and the inscriptions, the burials on this necropolis can be dated to the early third century B.C.E. Tomb 1 is richly decorated and includes a frieze of hunting scenes in which most of the animal portraits are accompanied by Greek labels.[30] A depiction of a lean giraffe, looking more like an

---

26. There is a possible hedgehog in the Praeneste mosaic, but its identification is far from certain. See Meyboom, *Nile Mosaic*, 24, 233 n. 46.

27. I. L. Seeligman's dating of the LXX Isaiah to the second century still remains the accepted opinion: *The Septuagint Version of Isaiah: A Discussion of Its Problems* (Mededelingen en verhandelingen van het Vooraziatisch–Egyptisch Genootschap "Ex Oriente Lux" 9; Leiden: Brill, 1948).

28. Meyboom, *Nile Mosaic*, 16–19.

29. The spelling is κ[α]μελοπάρ<δ>αλι[ς].

30. A. Kloner, "Maresha in the Reign of Ptolemy II Philadelphus," in *Ptolemy the Second Philadelphus and His World* (ed. P. R. McKechnie and P. Guillaume; Leiden: Brill, 2008), 171–82 (174–75).

alpaca than a camelopard, is accompanied by the label καμηλοπάρδαλις.[31] The similarities between the Nile mosaic and the Maresha hunting scene have long been noted and confirm the Egyptian nature of the hunt,[32] unsurprising given the Ptolemaic influence in Idumea.

The Praeneste and Maresha depictions of the giraffe have their own significance for the Septuagint. In Deuteronomy the giraffe is listed among permissible animals to eat:

ἔλαφον καὶ δορκάδα καὶ βούβαλον καὶ τραγέλαφον καὶ πύγαργον, ὄρυγα καὶ καμηλοπάρδαλιν (Deut 14:5)

deer and gazelle and roebuck and wild goat and white-rumped antelope and antelope and giraffe (NETS)

In this verse, καμηλοπάρδαλις is translating the Hebrew זמר, an uncertain animal that is understood to be a gazelle or animal that leaps (*HALOT* 274). The giraffe is not an animal native to Iron Age Palestine, nor is it an animal one would particularly think of eating. It was, however, known in Egypt and appears in Middle Kingdom reliefs, as it was brought from the southern Sudan as tribute to Egypt by Nubians.[33] The Praeneste mosaic confirms that in classical times it was seen as an exotic animal from Nubia, and the Egyptian influence in the Maresha paintings would support this. Agatharcides too reports that the camel is to be found in the region of the nomadic Troglodytes of Nubia.[34] That the Maresha artist clearly did not have precise knowledge of the anatomy of the beast further suggests that it was exotic and unfamiliar to Palestine. Interest in the animal might have been sparked by its inclusion in the grand procession to celebrate the accession of Ptolemy II (282–246 B.C.E., Athenaeus, *Deipnosophistai* 5.201), who wished to showcase the exotic animals and lands from within the Ptolemaic realm. It appears then that the giraffe is included as a kosher animal to actualize the Egyptian context or impart a certain exoticism to the list of animals. In similar fashion the Egyptian ibis is included as one of the inadmissible birds in Deut 14:16 where the Hebrew has תנשמת 'water-hen':

---

31. The name appears to be misspelt as ΚΑΜΕΛΟΠΑΡΔΑΛΟΣ. See J. P. Peters and H. Thiersch, *Painted Tombs in the Necropolis of Marissa (Marēshah)* (ed. S. A. Cook; London: Committee of the Palestine Exploration Fund, 1905), 25. For the errors in depiction of the giraffe, see Peters and Thiersch, *Painted Tombs*, 94; D. M. Jacobson, *The Hellenistic Paintings of Marisa* (Palestine Exploration Fund Annual 7; Leeds: Maney, 2007), 28–29.

32. Peters and Thiersch, *Painted Tombs*, xv–xvi. Jacobson, *Hellenistic Paintings*, 44, does point out that some of the animals are also native to the Levant.

33. See Meyboom, *Nile Mosaic*, 24.

34. Later traditions also place the giraffe in a variety of exotic places. See C. Hünemörder, "Giraffe," *Der Neue Pauly: Enzyklopädie der Antike* (ed. H. Cancik, H. Schneider, and M. Landfester; 16 vols.; Stuttgart: Metzler, 1996–2003), 4: 1075.

καὶ ἐρωδιὸν καὶ κύκνον καὶ ἶβιν

and heron and swan and ibis

It is possible that the translator did not know what the Hebrew words signified and therefore opted for a local flavor. Even so, keep a lookout for both animals; the giraffe might be easier to spot than an onocentaur.

2. Grammar

2.a. ἔναντι

The Greek word ἔναντι is one of a number of prepositions (cf. ἐνώπιον below) in the Septuagint that render the Hebrew half-prepositions.[35] Traditionally it was classed as one of a number of new prepositions chosen to render the Hebrew לִפְנֵי,[36] but many of these have been shown to have existed already in Koine, even if used with higher frequency in the Septuagint.[37] Sollamo says little about ἔναντι, presumably because it is a likely derivative of ἐναντίον, which is already well established in Greek.[38] For, ἔναντι is either a shortened form of ἐναντίον or a dialectal variant entering Greek in c. 300 B.C.E. from Crete, Delphi, or a similar dialect.[39] Wackernagel, who argues against Mayser's suggestion that it is a shortening of the longer preposition, points to the Cretan inscription with the spelling ἴναντι (context damaged):

Ἄκος | ἴναντι τõν εἰ (IKret II v 1 = GDI 5125a1)

The inscription is from the sixth or fifth century B.C.E., and the dialectal variation of ἰν for ἐν is well known (IG V 2.3.5). This certainly places the first use of this word much earlier than the Septuagint, but the one mere occurrence does not offer certainty as to its dialectal origin. For the spelling ἔναντι LSJ gives two epigraphic witnesses. The first, IG VII 2225.52 from Thibse in Euboea, is placed by LSJ in the second century B.C.E. and indeed it has been dated more precisely to 170 B.C.E. The second reference is not given a date in LSJ and is placed at the end of the entry. However,

---

35. The term of C. Brockelmann, *Grundriss der vergleichenden Grammatik der semitischen Sprachen* (2 vols.; Berlin: Reuther & Reichard, 1908–13), 2: § 243.

36. H. B. Swete, *An Introduction to the Old Testament in Greek with an Appendix Containing the Letter of Aristeas Edited by H. St. J. Thackeray* (rev. R. R. Ottley; Cambridge: Cambridge University Press, 1914), 306–9.

37. See R. Sollamo, "Some 'Improper' Prepositions, Such as ENΩΠΙΟΝ, ENANTION, ENANTI, Etc., in the Septuagint and Early Koine Greek," *VT* 25 (1975): 773–82.

38. Sollamo, "Some 'Improper' Prepositions," 780–81, on ἔναντι; 779–80, on ἐναντίον.

39. Sollamo, "Some 'Improper' Prepositions," 780–81. The dialectal origin is the suggestion of J. Wackernagel, *Hellenistica* (Göttingen: Kaestner, 1907), 3–6.

the Delphic inscription GDI 2072 (line 26) has been dated to 198 B.C.E., identifiable through the *strategos* named, Chalepos of Naupaktos who was active in the Fourth Macedonian war.[40] It therefore is an earlier occurrence, if not quite as early as the likely date of the Septuagint Pentateuch. The data in LSJ should be rearranged, nonetheless. One earlier example might exist of ἔναντι in a third-century B.C.E. inscription from Delphi, but it has been reconstructed at the crucial point: λαμβάνηι ἐναν[τι — — —].[41]

Overall the evidence from this sample is too slim to draw many conclusions. It is sufficient to note that the preposition is used in the inscriptions by the early second century and was therefore known in Koine. The translators of the Septuagint provide evidence of that early use and should not be seen as peculiar in their choice.

2.b. ἐνώπιον

Traditionally presented as an aspect of Jewish Greek,[42] the prepositional use of ἐνώπιον 'before, in the presence of' would be an apt choice for those with an awareness of the etymology of לִפְנֵי and who saw in ἐνώπιον the noun ὤψ 'face' plus a preposition. While the adjective ἐνώπιος exists earlier, it is the use specifically as a preposition (as a substitute for πρό) that is striking in biblical Greek. The use was soon noticed in documentary material as they began to be published. Deissmann cited BGU 2.578 (TM 9238; 189 C.E.), but this late papyrus only attests to an adverbial use from which Deissmann derived the Septuagint prepositional use.[43] It is improbable that it is derived from the adverbial use. He also refers to P.Grenf. I 38.11 (TM 262), which Grenfell dated to the second or first century B.C.E. (more precisely 170 B.C.E.).[44] LSJ (579) also provide documentary evidence: P.Cair.Zen. 73.14 (= 1.59073.13 [TM 728]; third century B.C.E.) and P.Grenf. I 38.11 (as Deissmann). The papyri exhibit a number of examples, but almost all are in damaged contexts, rendering reconstruction difficult. Even in P.Cair.Zen. 1.59073.13 the preposition is

---

40. J. D. Grainger, *The League of the Aitolians* (Mnemosyne, bibliotheca classica Batava. Supplementum 200; Leiden: Brill, 1999), 371.

41. J. Bousquet, "Inscriptions de Delphes," *BCH* 88 (1964): 380–94 (382).

42. For examples see G. A. Deissmann, *Bible Studies: Contributions, Chiefly from Papyri and Inscriptions, to the History of the Language, the Literature, and the Religion of Hellenistic Judaism and Primitive Christianity* (Edinburgh: T. & T. Clark, 1909), 213.

43. *Bible Studies*, 213; cf. E. J. Bickerman, "The Septuagint as a Translation," *PAAJR* 28 (1959): 1–39 (13).

44. B. P. Grenfell, *An Alexandrian Erotic Fragment and Other Greek Papyri Chiefly Ptolemaic* (Oxford: Clarendon, 1896), 70. On date see *Berichtigungsliste der griechischen Papyrusurkunden aus Ägypten* (ed. F. A. J. Hoogendijk, M. J. Bakker, N. Kruit, and A. V. Bakkers; Berlin: Vereinigung Wissenschaftlicher Verleger, 1922–), 3: 70.

well preserved but the genitive ending on the following noun has been lost. Nonetheless, the papyri do show its legal use in actions performed in the presence of someone or for them personally.[45]

Inscriptions provide further examples of this prepositional use and in some cases the text is better preserved for comparison. The earliest example is from Epidauros (fourth/early third century B.C.E.):

καστον τετόρων ὀβολῶ[ν — — — — — — — — — — — — — —]
ἐγώπιον παραστασί[ων — — — — — — — — — — — — — λόγο]-
(SEG 25:392.25–26)

The lack of context and the uncertainty of the reading of some letters of ἐνώπιον do not inspire much confidence. However, in a series of manumission records from Thessaly, we find a phrase repeated many times, in reference to the distribution of property:[46]

ἠρίθμησεν ἐνώπιον κοινοῦ ξενοδόκου

he counted in the presence of a public witness

In some cases the text is damaged, but the regularity of the formula allows for easy reconstruction. The inscriptions have been dated paleographically to the early second century B.C.E. (e.g., SEG 35:593). These inscriptions provide clear evidence of the usage from the same time period as the Septuagint. The Septuagint is clearly more varied in its use, but chance survival has preserved only legal uses in the papyri and inscriptions.[47]

2.c. υἱός

The biblical use of υἱός followed by genitive to express an adjectival concept has naturally been seen as a Hebraism by many: for example, υἱοὶ ἀδικίας (2 Kdgms 7:10); υἱοὶ θανατώσεως (1 Kdgms 26:16).[48] Deissmann saw this type of expression as a translation feature more than a linguistic tendency, but nonetheless was able to summon up examples from coins and inscriptions in defense of the Greek. As this work by Deissmann has

---

45. Sollamo, "Some 'Improper' Prepositions," 777. Hogeterp briefly surveys the evidence for ἐνώπιον, but restricts himself to papyri and literature, and not the inscriptions (A. L. A. Hogeterp, "New Testament Greek as Popular Speech: Adolf Deissmann in Retrospect: A Case Study in Luke's Greek," *ZNW* 102 [2011]: 178–200 [190–92]).

46. E.g., *BCH* 95 (1971) 562.16, 19; SEG 29:532.8, 11, 14, 17; SEG 35:593.5, and SEG 35:593[1].5.

47. So Sollamo, "Some 'Improper' Prepositions," 778. The temporal use is the result of lexical stereotyping in the Septuagint, though (779).

48. For examples of scholarly views, see Deissmann, *Bible Studies*, 161. See too LSJ 1846–47.

been recently supplemented by further examples, all that need be noted here is the confirmation of this type of construction. Deissmann drew attention to honorific titles in inscriptions comprising υἱός and a noun denoting their role or position: υἱὸς τῆς γερουσίας, υἱὸς τῆς πόλεως, and υἱὸς τοῦ δήμου.[49] New collections of the evidence for υἱὸς τῆς πόλεως have now appeared and it has been subjected to a detailed investigation.[50] The expression indicates that elite members were adopted by the city as a reward for services rendered. It is only partially comparable to the Septuagint usage, and seems to be primarily an Imperial term in specific contexts. It demonstrates the flexibility of the word υἱός, and the reason why the Septuagint could adapt it in Greek, but it must be admitted that the usage of the Septuagint remains odd.

3. Register

Inscriptions cover a wider array of genres and styles than papyri and therefore afford opportunity for testing theories of the register of particular words. A range of considerations have to be taken into account when determining register, but the appearance of words only in certain types of inscription is a strong indicator. The first example, βῶλαξ, illustrates this well.

3.a. βῶλαξ

The noun βῶλαξ meaning a 'clod of earth' would seem to be of little value in its one appearance in the Septuagint:[51]

φύρεται δέ μου τὸ σῶμα ἐν σαπρίᾳ σκωλήκων,
τήκω δὲ βώλακας γῆς ἀπὸ ἰχῶρος ξύων (Job 7:5)

my body is spoiled in the decay of worms
and I waste away, scraping clods of earth from the pus

In this pericope Job emphasizes the human condition and his own mortality, typified by his physical condition. The Greek expression "clods of earth" is a translation of the Qere reading in the Hebrew Masoretic text,

---

49. *Bible Studies,* 16–66.
50. A. Laronde, "Huios tès poléôs," in *Cyrène à Catherine. Trois mille ans de Libyennes. Études grecques et latines offertes à Catherine Dobias Lalou* (ed. F. Poli and G. Vottéro; Nancy: A.D.R.A., 2005), 149–59; F. Canali De Rossi, *Filius Publicus: Huios tês poleos e titoli affini in iscrizioni greche di età imperial. Studi sul vocabulario dell'evergesia* 1 (Rome: Herder, 2007); SEG 55:2117. Cf. Hogeterp, "New Testament Greek," 186–90.
51. LXX reference added to the LSJ data by R. Renehan, *Greek Lexicographical Notes: A Critical Supplement to the Greek-English Lexicon of Liddell-Scott-Jones* (Hypomnemata 45; Göttingen: Vandenhoeck & Ruprecht, 1975), 56.

explained as the crust of earth, figuratively denoting a scab.[52] Job expresses his condition in terms of worms and earth, symbolic of the grave.[53]

The Septuagint choice can be used as a good illustration of how to determine register. The noun βῶλαξ appears to be a poetic variant of βῶλος, the suffix -αξ chosen perhaps as an archaic form for the purposes of poetic composition, one of a number of similar internal derivations in Greek (cf. δίφραξ from δίφρος).[54] In this case the existence in Homer of ἐριβῶλαξ 'with large clods; very fertile' as a by-form of ἐρίβωλος might suggest either an archaic origin or modelling upon the Homeric word. The form βῶλαξ is attested before the Septuagint in Pindar (*Pyth.* 4.37), Theocritus (*Id.* 17.80) and Apollonius Rhodius (*Arg.* 3.1334; 4.1562, 1750), each of them poets who modelled their style on Homer. In Pindar βῶλαξ denotes the earth given by the gods, in Theocritus the land watered by the Nile, and in Apollonius actual clods of earth turned up by ploughing (*Arg.* 3.1334) as well as clods of earth presented as an offering (*Arg.* 4.1562, 1750).[55]

The fact that βῶλαξ is entirely absent from the documentary papyri supports the supposition that it is a rare and high word. Its presence in three inscriptions, geographically ranging from mainland Greece to the eastern border of modern Romania, is proof, however, that it would have been known to educated writers and was adopted for poetic expressions[56]—all three inscriptions are poetic funerary epitaphs, combining dialectal and poetic forms. Consider the opening of one of them, an inscription from the first century c.e., from the island of Paros, found in the ancient necropolis adjacent to Hekatontapyliane (IG XII 5.307). This is the fifth of a number of inscriptions on a sarcophagus, found on the upper right corner:

5.1   τίς σε, γύναι, Παρίην ὑπὸ βώλακα θήκατο; τίς σο[ι]
       ξυνὸν ὑπὲρ τύμβου σᾶμα τόδ᾽ ἀγλάϊσεν;[57]

---

52. E. Dhorme, *A Commentary on the Book of Job. Translated by Harold Knight, with a Prefatory Note by H. H. Rowley* (London: Thomas Nelson, 1967); J. Gray, *The Book of Job* (ed. D. J. A. Clines; The text of the Hebrew Bible 1; Sheffield: Sheffield Phoenix, 2010), 179; G. R. Driver, "Problems in the Hebrew Text of Job," *Wisdom in Israel and in the Ancient Near East* (ed. M. Noth and D. Winton Thomas; VTSup 3; Leiden: Brill, 1960), 72–93 (73–76).

53. N. C. Habel, *The Book of Job: A Commentary* (Philadelphia: Westminster, 1985), 157.

54. P. Chantraine, *La Formation des noms en grec ancient* (Paris: Champion, 1933), 379.

55. There is a variation between βῶλος in *Arg.* 4.1552 and βῶλαξ in *Arg.* 4.1562, both with the same referent.

56. IG IV² 1.35 (no date, Epidauros); IScM II 166 (first century b.c.e., Tomis [Constanṭa]); IG XII 5.307 (first century c.e., Paros).

57. W. Peek, *Griechische Vers-Inschriften, 1. Grab-Epigramme* (Berlin: Akademie-Verlag, 1955), 1860. A brief introduction and translation is provided by D. Clay, *Archilochos*

Who placed you, Lady, beneath the earth of Paros? Who has
adorned for yo[u] this shared memorial over your grave?

Comparable to the word's appearance in the Hellenistic poets, it is here
found in a metrical inscription, with obvious Doric forms such as σᾶμα for
σῆμα, and Lyric ξυνός for κοινός. Earlier from the first century B.C.E., an
inscription speaks in similar fashion of the deceased as lying "beneath the
mournful earth" (ὑπὸ βώλακα κεῖνται, IScM II 166.1; cf. IG IV² 1.35). It
thus can be seen that βῶλαξ only appears in literary works and inscriptions,
and should be seen as part of a higher register.

3.b. νέφος

Examination of the appearances of νέφος 'cloud' in the Septuagint
suggests it is a poetic term serving as a synonym for νεφέλη. It appears
only in books that show a tendency towards creativity or the use of poetic
vocabulary: Psalms (once), Proverbs (five times), Ecclesiastes (twice), Job
(17 times),[58] and Wisdom (once).[59] This is not surprising when it appears
frequently in Homer and was adopted by the classical poets, and yet is not
common in prose writers (LSJ 1171). Little can be determined on a statis-
tical basis from documentary sources. Consultation of the papyri indicates
there that there are no occurrences of the word at all, but also that there
are no occurrences of νεφέλη either. Therefore it might be the content of
documentary papyri that excludes discussion of clouds more than evidence
of the register.

Nonetheless, some differentiation can be seen in the inscriptions. The
common form νεφέλη is found in two inscriptions, one from third-century B.C.E. Miletus (IMiletMcCabe 470),[60] and one from first-century C.E.
Egypt (IEgVers 115 [TM 107215]).[61] They are both literary in nature, the
Miletus inscription being a funeral epitaph in elegiacs and the Egyptian
one a metrical hymn. The synonym νέφος appears in three inscriptions

---

Heros: The Cult of Poets in the Greek Polis (Hellenic Studies 6; Cambridge, MA: Harvard
University Press, 2004), 33–34; and a transcription, 124.

58. A number of these are found in asterisked material, but the majority are in OG.

59. The majority of these books are classified as "literary" Greek by H. St. J. Thackeray,
A Grammar of the Old Testament in Greek according to the Septuagint (Cambridge: Cambridge University Press, 1909), 13. Psalms is portrayed by him as "indifferent," reflecting
the translation style, but not taking into account its distinctive and at times poetic language.
Ecclesiastes might seem out of place in such a list, but see J. K. Aitken, "Rhetoric and Poetry
in Greek Ecclesiastes," *BIOSCS* 38 (2005): 55–78.

60. W. Peek, "Milesische Versinschriften," *ZPE* 7 (1971): 193–226 (216).

61. The similarity in content of IEgVers 114 (TM 104054) suggests it too contained
the word, but the stone is damaged at the corresponding part.

before the time of Hadrian, each of them metrical,[62] and continues in later inscriptions. This evidence is slim for deriving conclusions, and it is possible that it is only in poetic texts that clouds would be mentioned. Nevertheless, the fact that the rare form νέφος is as frequent as the common form and we find it only in poetic texts is corroborating data for interpreting it as a poetic term when used in the Septuagint.

3.c. πάντοτε

The temporal adverb πάντοτε is only found in the Septuagint in the literary Greek of Wisdom of Solomon (Wis 11:21; 19:18). It is already known in the fourth century in the comic Philemon, Aristotle, and Menander.[63] Although condemned by Atticists in favor of διαπαντός or ἑκάστοτε (Phrynichus 82),[64] it still might reflect a higher register. It is not found in papyri, but in its one appearance in inscriptions it is in verse. The unlikely location of the poem is a graffito in the toilet at Ephesus, dated to the fourth century B.C.E.:

> ἂν μή γ' ἔλωμεν τὸν βίον τὸν δραπέτην
> πινῶντες ἢ τρυφῶντες ἢ λελουμένοι,
> ὀδύνην ἑαυτοῖς προξενοῦμεν πάντοτε
> ἀναξίους ὁρῶντες εὐτυχεστέρους.[65]

> If we had not grasped life, the fugitive
> Drinking or feasting or bathing
> We procure for ourselves <u>endless</u> pain
> Seeing worthless people being more fortunate

This toilet philosopher was perhaps not as creative as he seems since a very similar poetic aphorism appears in the *Greek Anthology* (*AP* 10.87), reading the preferable γελῶμεν instead of γ' ἔλωμεν.[66] Both sources confirm the use of this form in literary Greek, if we ignore the unfortunate location of the inscription.

---

62. IG IX 1² 2.340 (second to first century B.C.E.), SEG 54:788 (second to first century B.C.E.), and IG XII 5.739 (reign of Augustus).

63. LSJ 1300–1.

64. R. Renehan, *Greek Lexicographical Notes: A Critical Supplement to the Greek-English Lexicon of Liddell-Scott-Jones. Series 2* (Hypomnemata 74; Göttingen: Vandenhoeck & Ruprecht, 1982), 112–13.

65. IEph 456.2. First published by R. Heberdey, "Vorläufige Berichte über die Ausgrabungen in Ephesus," *JÖAI* 1 Beiblatt (1898): 54–82 (75 no. II).

66. "If we do not laugh at life the runaway . . ." Discussed by R. Weisshäupl, "Ephesische Latrinen-Inschriften," *JÖAI* 5 Beiblatt (1902): 33–34 no. II.

3.d. τοιγαροῦν

As a particle τοιγαροῦν 'therefore' is perhaps unsurprisingly not often found in the pages of the Septuagint. Apart from the Greek compositions of 2 Maccabees (7:23) and 4 Maccabees (1:34; 9:7; 13:16; 17:4), it is only found in the more literary translations of Isaiah (5:26), Proverbs (1:26, 31), Job (22:10; 24:22), and Sirach (41:16).[67] In the majority of these appearances there is merely a *waw* in the preserved Hebrew MT,[68] which would more often be translated by a καί or δέ. Only at Job 22:10 is there an equivalent Hebrew particle על־כן. From the perspective of translation technique τοιγαροῦν normally takes initial position in the sentence and therefore matches the word order of the Hebrew where *waw* or על־כן are also in initial position. In choosing τοιγαροῦν the translators have selected a strongly emphatic particle, but one whose strength is weakening in this time period. Its weakening is seen in its placement occasionally second in the sentence, such as in a second-century C.E. inscription: βούλομαι τοιγαροῦν τούτου τοῦ μνημείου.[69] It is notable that in the one of the latest works of the Septuagint it is to be found in second position (e.g., 4 Macc 9:7; 13:16; 17:4, from the first or second centuries C.E.). Its popularity in the Hellenistic and Roman periods is evident from its frequency in such writers as Polybius, Josephus, Philo, Plutarch, Epictetus, and Dio Chrysostom, being favored among late Hellenistic writers owing to the weakening in its strength.[70]

The appearance of the particle in Proverbs is an example of this weakening. Cook remarks that the use of particles in chapter 1 is indicative of the creative style of the translator.[71] The repetition in close succession of τοιγαροῦν (Prov 1:26, 31) would appear to be heavy and not literary,[72] although the weakening might allow for this:

---

67. This is following Thackeray's categorisation of Septuagint books (*Grammar*, 13) except for placing Sirach among the literary translations too. For the literary character of Sirach see J. K. Aitken, "The Literary Attainment of the Translator of Greek Sirach," in *The Texts and Versions of the Book of Ben Sira: Transmission and Interpretation* (ed. J.-S. Rey and J. Joosten; Leiden: Brill, 2011), 95–126.

68. At Sir 41:16 there does not appear to be an equivalent to the particle in the Hebrew of MS B or Masada. J. Cook, *The Septuagint of Proverbs: Jewish and/or Hellenistic Proverbs? Concerning the Hellenistic Colouring of LXX Proverbs* (VTSup 69; Leiden: Brill, 1997), 89, suggests that at Prov 1:26 τοιγαροῦν renders Hebrew גם, but it is possible the whole phrase גם־אני is encapsulated in κἀγώ. Therefore there also would be no equivalent for τοιγαροῦν there.

69. P. Herrmann and K. Z. Polatkan, *Das Testament des Epikrates und andere neue Inschriften aus dem Museum von Manisa* (Vienna: Hermann Böhlaus Nachfolger, 1969), 7, 1.

70. Cf. Aitken, "Literary Attainment," 114.

71. Cook, *Septuagint of Proverbs*, 103–4.

72. Cf. J. K. Aitken, "The Language of the Septuagint: Recent Theories, Future Prospects," *BJGS* 24 (1999): 24–33 (28–29).

26 <u>τοιγαροῦν</u> κἀγὼ τῇ ὑμετέρᾳ ἀπωλείᾳ ἐπιγελάσομαι . . .

Therefore I in turn will also laugh at your destruction . . .

31 <u>τοιγαροῦν</u> ἔδονται τῆς ἑαυτῶν ὁδοῦ τοὺς καρπούς

Therefore they shall eat the fruits of their own way

A remarkable parallel to this can in fact be found in an Isis aretalogy preserved on a marble stele from Thrace, dated to the mid-second to early first century B.C.E. The language is literary and poetic:

<u>τοι</u>|[<u>γα</u>]<u>ροῦν</u> αἱ πόλεις εὐστάθησαν, οὐ τὴν βίαν νομικὸν ἀλλὰ | [τ]ὸν νόμον ἀβίαστον εὑροῦσαι. σὺ τιμᾶσθαι γονεῖς ὑπὸ | [τ]έκνων ἐποίησας, οὐ μόνον ὡς πατέρων, ἀλλ᾽ ὡς καὶ θεῶν | [φ]ροντίσασα· <u>τοιγαροῦν</u> ἡ χάρις κρείσσων ὅτε τῆς φύσε|ως τὴν ἀνάγκην καὶ θεὰ νόμον ἔγραψεν. (SEG 26:821.29–33)[73]

The[re]fore the cities enjoy peace, discovering not the violence enshrined in law, but law without violence. You have made it that parents are honored by their [ch]ildren, not only [th]inking of them as parents, but even as gods. Therefore the good will is greater when it is a goddess who has written the law out of natural necessity.

A third τοιγαροῦν appears in line 38 after a similar interval. Succession of correlative conjunctions is not unknown, even in threes as in this inscription. In Proverbs 1 we also find the triple use of τε (Prov 1:2–3), and that is a phenomenon recognized in classical authors.[74] However, the close succession of the particle τοιγαροῦν is uncommon. This literary inscription from the same period as the Septuagint indicates it could be used by a literary author and we need not be so surprised by the example from Proverbs. As a particle expected in a higher register, τοιγαροῦν appears primarily in very late papyri and inscriptions. Its distribution in the Septuagint, attested only in 2 Maccabees, 4 Maccabees, Proverbs, Job, and Isaiah, testifies to its use particularly in the literary translations or compositions. The Isis aretalogy shows that the repeated appearance in Proverbs 1 is not a departure from its literary sensibilities.

---

73. See too Y. Grandjean, *Une nouvelle Arétalogie d'Isis à Maronée* (Études préliminaires aux religions orientales dans l'Empire romain 49; Leiden: Brill, 1975).

74. J. D. Denniston, *The Greek Particles* (2nd ed.; Oxford: Clarendon Press, 1954), 504–5.

CHAPTER 6

Geographical Distribution

Regional variation in Koine is one of the hardest features to prove, especially given the lack of data for comparison on the scale of that from Egypt. The dominance of papyri in the discussion of biblical Greek has necessarily limited the scope we consider, but this is where the inscriptions have a great advantage, coming as they do from different regions. While consideration has been given to the possibility that some Septuagint translations originated from locations other than Egypt, rarely is linguistic evidence brought up in support of such theories.[1] Theoretically, it should be possible that there was dialectal variation in Koine, since the language was spread across a very wide region and was spoken by diverse peoples whose native tongue itself varied considerably. Regional dialects in modern Greek, such as Pontic or Cappadocian, indicate that this is possible. The attempts to identify actual regional differences in Koine, however, have been few.[2]

One difficulty in determining lexical variation is that even a word that has a regional origin can easily be adopted into the language and used elsewhere. The Ptolemies themselves did not limit their empire to Egypt or restrict their contact with others, allowing even apparently Egyptian-provenance words to spread.[3] Nevertheless, the continuance of classical dialects

---

1. See the comments by S. A. Adams, "Review of J. Cook and A. van der Kooij, *Law, Prophets, and Wisdom: On the Provenance of Translators and Their Books in the Septuagint Version* (CBET 68; Leuven: Peeters, 2012)," *RBL* 8/2013 [online: www.bookreviews.org] (2013): "Moreover, it would have been beneficial (since it was brought up) to evaluate the possible Greek linguistic differences between Egypt and Judea to determine if there was any further internal support for a Jerusalem origin."

2. See, e.g., V. Bubeník, *Hellenistic and Roman Greece as a Sociolinguistic Area* (Amsterdam Studies in the Theory and History of Linguistic Science IV; Current Issues in Linguistic Theory 57; Amsterdam: Benjamins, 1989); S.-T. Teodorsson, "Phonological Variation in Classical Attic and the Development of Koine," *Glotta* 57 (1979): 61–75.

3. R. S. Bagnall, *The Administration of the Ptolemaic Possessions Outside Egypt* (Columbia Studies in the Classical Tradition 4; Leiden: Brill, 1976); A. Meadows, "Ptolemaic Possessions outside Egypt," in *The Encyclopedia of Ancient History* (ed. R. S. Bagnall, K. Brodersen, C. B. Champion, A. Erskine, and S. R. Huebner; London: Blackwell, 2013), 5625–29. See now the collection of essays in *The Ptolemies, the Sea and the Nile: Studies in*

through the Hellenistic and Roman period might also have had an influence too. At the least they indicate regional variation. Thus, while Koine had penetrated Lesbos by the mid-fourth century as shown by inscriptions in Koine (IG XII 2.3 from c. 360 B.C.E.;[4] IG XII 2.10; 2.11 from c. 330 [5]), local Aeolic still continued in use (e.g., IG XII 2.15, c. 214–213) and Aeolic elements can still be found as late as the early Roman Empire.[6] Many inscriptions are still written in Doric as a language of poetry, even by Jews in Egypt (*JIGRE* 38 [TM 6271]). There was an awareness of language differences in the Hellenistic period too. Clarysse recalls Theocritus's 15th Idyll (87–95) where two Syracusan women, on being asked to stop "babbling like wood pigeons," declare, "Peloponnesian is what we are talking. Dorians may, I suppose, be permitted to speak Dorian (Δωρίσδειν δ᾽ ἔξεστι, δοκῶ, τοῖς Δωριέεσσι)."[7] Roman period awareness of local levels of language is implied by Sextus Empiricus's quotation (second century C.E.) of a lost Aristophanic comedy (K–A 706), which he uses as evidence that "the ancient Athenian idiom is different again from the modern one, and the idiom of those who live in rural areas is different from that of city dwellers."[8] How far we can derive much of substance from this, though, is clearly an issue. Meanwhile, an earlier generation did tend to identify oddities in Greek of the papyri as attributable to Egyptian speakers, but with growing knowledge of Koine in papyri this conclusion can often be discounted.[9] Even Egyptian loanwords need not necessarily indicate Egyptian provenance.

Regional differences might be identified in lexical choice in the Septuagint if it can be shown that the translated books derive from different

---

Waterborne Power (ed. K. Buraselis, M. Stefanou, and D. J. Thompson; Cambridge: Cambridge University Press, 2013), and especially the essay by Andrew Meadows, "The Ptolemaic League of Islanders," 19–38.

4. A. J. Heisserer, "IG XII, 2, 1. (The Monetary Pact between Mytilene and Phokaia)," *ZPE* 55 (1984): 115–32.

5. Cf. A. J. Heisserer, "Observations on 'IG' XII 2, 10 and 11," *ZPE* 74 (1988): 111–32 (119).

6. R. Hodot, "Le décret de Kymè en l'honneur de Labéon," *ZPE* 19 (1975): 121–33; R. Hodot, "Décret de Kymè en l'honneur du prytane Kléanax," *J. Paul Getty Museum Journal* 10 (1982): 165–80.

7. W. Clarysse, "Ethnic Diversity and Dialect among the Greeks of Hellenistic Egypt," in *The Two Faces of Graeco-Roman Egypt. Greek and Demotic and Greek-Demotic Texts and Studies Presented to P. W. Pestman* (ed. A. M. F. W. Verhoogt and S. P. Vleeming; Papyrologica Lugduno-Batava 30; Leiden: Brill, 1998), 1–13 (5).

8. For discussion see S. Colvin, "The Language of Non-Athenians in Old Comedy," in *The Rivals of Aristophanes* (ed. D. Harvey and J. Wilkins; London: Duckworth, 2000), 285–98 (290). My thanks to Dr. Patrick James for drawing my attention to this citation.

9. See T. V. Evans, "Complaints of the Natives in a Greek Dress: The Zenon Archive and the Problem of Egyptian Interference," in *Multilingualism in the Graeco-Roman Worlds* (ed. A. Mullen and P. James; Cambridge: Cambridge University Press, 2012), 106–23.

parts of the Mediterranean rather than from Egypt, or if a word could be seen as distinctively Egyptian, despite the above caveats. There has, for instance, been considerable debate regarding the translation of the Psalms, while the epilogue to Esther implies a Jerusalem connection.[10] *Kaige* texts might also derive from Palestine (Canticles, Ruth, Lamentations and 1 Esdras) as might Ecclesiastes owing to its style being close to that of the second-century reviser Aquila. It has been suggested that other translations such as Proverbs, Judith, Daniel, and Tobit could derive from Judea. Nevertheless, the distance between Palestine and Egypt is small and they were under the same Ptolemaic Empire for a time so that we cannot be certain of a distinct language difference between them. Further afield a case has been made for Asia Minor as the provenance of the Greek composition *The Third Sibylline Oracle*, which mentions Asia frequently,[11] but this is not beyond dispute. It is possible then that inscriptions could throw some light on this problem in either of two directions. First, if it can be shown that certain words are found in a specific region, then inscriptions provide support for a non-Egyptian provenance, especially in those cases where the papyri have been relied on exclusively. Second, and by contrast, if a word is found only in papyri and not in inscriptions outside Egypt this will corroborate apparent Egyptian features already identified.[12]

One well-known case of a term called too easily in support of an Egyptian provenance is that of the Greek βᾶρις (and consequently πυργόβαρις).[13] Jerome (*Letter* 65 = PL 22.633) records that βᾶρις is only used in Palestine with a particular sense of 'fortress' ("*verbum sit ἐπιχώριον Palestinae*") and

---

10. Full discussion of the location of translations can be found in E. Tov, "Reflections on the Septuagint with Special Attention Paid to the Post-Pentateuchal Translations," in *Die Septuaginta—Texte, Theologien, Einflüsse; 2. internationale Fachtagung veranstaltet von Septuaginta Deutsch (LXX.D), Wuppertal 23.–27.7. 2008* (ed. W. Kraus and M. Karrer; WUNT 252; Tübingen: Mohr Siebeck, 2010), 3–22. See too J. Cook and A. van der Kooij, *Law, Prophets, and Wisdom: On the Provenance of Translators and Their Books in the Septuagint Version* (CBET 68; Leuven: Peeters, 2012).

11. R. Buitenwerf, *Book III of the Sibylline Oracles and Its Social Setting, with an Introduction, Translation and Commentary* (Studia in Veteris Testamenti pseudepigrapha 17; Leiden: Brill, 2003).

12. For other Egyptian features, see J. Joosten, "The Septuagint as a Source of Information on Egyptian Aramaic in the Hellenistic Period," in *Aramaic in Its Historical and Linguistic Setting* (ed. H. Gzella and M. L. Folmer; Veröffentlichungen der Orientalistischen Kommission 50; Wiesbaden: Harrassowitz, 2008), 93–105; J. Joosten, "To See God. Conflicting Exegetical Tendencies in the Septuagint," in *Die Septuaginta - Texte, Kontexte, Lebenswelten* (ed. M. Karrer and W. Kraus; WUNT 219; Tübingen: Mohr Siebeck, 2008), 287–99.

13. H.-J. Venetz, *Quinta des Psalteriums: ein Beitrag zur Septuaginta- und Hexaplaforschung* (Collection Massorah 1; Études classiques et texts 2; Hildesheim: Gerstenberg, 1974). See A. van der Kooij, "On the Place of Origin of the Old Greek of Psalms," *VT* 33 (1983): 67–74 (70–71).

that elsewhere it denotes a type of 'boat.' LSJ (307), nevertheless, gives both homonyms as deriving from Egypt. Van der Kooij argues that since βᾶρις denotes a 'boat' in Egypt, βᾶρις in the Septuagint would have been misunderstood there, and that this is additional evidence that the LXX Psalter was translated in Palestine and not Egypt.[14] He suggests that βᾶρις meaning 'fortress' is found only in inscriptions from Laodicea, in Josephus, and in Septuagint texts of the *kai gar* and *kaige* groups.[15] In response Pietersma, noting that homonyms are not always distinguished by geographical location, argues that one cannot use one such a word as a basis for a location when other words could provide counter-evidence.[16] The inscriptions can contribute significantly to this debate. Indeed the presence of the term in inscriptions from outside Palestine[17] should already have alerted van der Kooij to the possibility that this is not a distinctly Palestinian use of the term. The inscriptions concerned are in fact not from Laodicea, as van der Kooij states, but from Didyma on the Ionian coast. The word appears five times in this set of documents, all published together on a stele from the temple of Apollo, and dating from the year 253 B.C.E. in the reign of Antiochus II. One (OGIS 225.33–50) is a dossier concerning the sale of the village of Pannucome (northwestern Turkey) by Antiochus II to his wife or former wife Laodice. It is therefore known as the Laodice inscription, and hence the confusion with Laodicea. This decree specifies the property to be exchanged as:[18]

[. . . . .] Πάννο[υ κώμη]
[καὶ ἡ βᾶρις καὶ ἡ χώρα καὶ οἱ ὑπάρχοντε]ς λα[οί· (OGIS 225.54–55)
. . . Pannu[come and the manor house and the land belonging to it and the] peasants [who live there

These details are repeated further down the decree:

ἥ τε κώμη καὶ ἡ βᾶρις καὶ ἡ προσοῦσ[α χώ]|[ρα] (OGIS 225.56–57)
the village, the manor house and the [land] belongi[ng] to it

---

14. Van der Kooij, "On the Place of Origin," 70–71.

15. Van der Kooij, "On the Place of Origin," 70.

16. A. Pietersma, "The Place of Origin of the Old Greek Psalter," in *The World of the Aramaeans I. Biblical Studies in Honour of Paul-Eugène Dion* (ed. P. M. Michèle Daviau, J. W. Wevers, and M. Weigl; Sheffield: Sheffield Academic, 2001), 252–74 (253).

17. For these inscriptions, van der Kooij refers to H. Kreissig, *Wirtschaft und Gesellschaft im Seleukidenreich: die Eigentums- und die Abhängigkeitsverhältnisse* (Schriften zur Geschichte und Kultur der Antike 16; Berlin: Akademie-Verlag, 1978), 23.

18. First published by A. Rehm, *Didyma II: Die Inschriften* (Berlin: Mann, 1958), 492c. Republished in C. B. Welles, *Royal Correspondence in the Hellenistic Period: A Study in Greek Epigraphy* (New Haven: Yale University Press, 1934), no. 20. See too SEG 19:676.

Here Welles has translated βᾶρις as manor house in an attempt to understand it in the context.[19] It is clearly an architectural structure, nonetheless. Although the text has been partially reconstructed in this example, the reading is certain from the reference to the same agreement beginning a letter of Antiochus II to his general Metrophanes, preserved on the same stele (OGIS 225.1–33).[20]

Δαισίου. Βασιλεὺς Ἀντίοχος Μητροφάνει χαίρειν. πεπ[ρά]-
καμεν Λαοδίκηι Πάννου κώμην καὶ τὴν βᾶριν καὶ τὴν προσο[ῦ]-
σαν χώραν τῆι κώμηι

King Antiochus to Metrophanes, greeting. We hav[e so]ld to Laodice Pannucome and the manor house and the land belo[ng]ing to the village

These examples show the noun βᾶρις denoting most probably a country estate in a location far from Palestine and confirm the inaccuracy of Jerome's statement. One further example in another location is found from the first to second century C.E. in Apollonia (modern Sozopol), Bulgaria:[21]

Μητοκος Ταρουλου φύσι δὲ
Δέκμου κτίσας τὴν πόλιν
μετὰ τὴν ἔκπτωσιν καὶ ἐ-
πισσκευάσας {ἐπισκευάσας} τὸ τρίπυλον
καὶ τὴν βᾶριν Ἀπόλλωνι Ἰητρ[ῷ].

Metokos, son of Taroulus and the natural son of Dekmos, having founded the city after devastation and repaired the triple gate and the fortress, (dedicated it) to Apollo Ietr[os].

Since βᾶρις meaning a boat is most likely an Egyptian loanword,[22] Jerome should have argued in the opposite direction: not βᾶρις 'tower' as typical of Palestine, but βᾶρις 'boat' as typical of Egypt. Even then if βᾶρις 'tower' was widely used in Greek, there would have been no confusion over the meaning of the Psalms in Egypt.

This example shows how difficult it is to determine geographical specificity and how the distribution of inscriptions allows for correction of

19. Welles, *Royal Correspondence*, 103; cf. 320–21, where he calls βᾶρις a manor house, following Rostovtzeff, but then offers a linguistic history that shows it refers to a fortified structure that could be part of a manor house.

20. Rehm, *Didyma II*, 492b; Welles, *Royal Correspondence*, no. 18.

21. *Inscriptiones graecae in Bulgaria repertae, Vol. 1: Inscriptiones orae Ponti Euxini* (ed. G. Mihailov; 2nd ed.; Sofia: In aedibus typographicis Academiae Litterarum Bulgaricae, 1970), no. 400.

22. So Welles, *Royal Correspondence*, 320; *EDG* 1: 202; B. Hemmerdinger, "Noms communs grecs d'origine égyptienne," *Glotta* 46 (1968): 238–47 (241).

previous suppositions. To broaden the dataset beyond the one word βᾶρις, Pietersma drew attention to additional words that could be indicative of an Egyptian setting. He focused on papyri, but since the majority of these are from Egypt, they cannot be used to identify a word as Egyptian in provenance, exclusive of other evidence.[23] Deissmann had himself early on warned against the view of an Egyptian Greek, concluding that local differences in Greek were insignificant.[24] In this he might have been reacting too strongly against a prevailing opinion, as distinct local differences could well have existed. Nevertheless, the point is well made that a good case must be made if one is to argue for a regional vocabulary. We begin with three relatively straightforward examples of negative evidence that inscriptions can provide before moving to more complex cases where a regional coloring might be suggested.

1. ἀντιλήμπτωρ

Attention has already been drawn to the case of the noun ἀντιλήμπτωρ, which Deissmann identified in a papyrus as a term from the secular domain transferred to the domain of divine terminology in the Bible.[25] The term ἀντιλήμπτωρ 'helper, protector' (LSJ 158) appears in addresses to God twenty times in the Septuagint (sixteen times in the Psalms) and once in 1 Enoch before becoming a popular term in Christian sources:

ἀντιλήμπτωρ μου εἶ καὶ καταφυγή μου (Ps 90:2)

You are my helper and my refuge

Deissmann at the time only knew of one occurrence, but many more have since come to light. The finds from papyri have shown that ἀντιλήμπτωρ was the designation of the Ptolemaic king or another official of the Ptolemaic and Roman periods. The term was used when people would appeal

---

23. Note how often Pietersma, "Place of Origin," for example, speaks of "Egyptian papyri" without attention to this circular argument (270): ἀναφορά, "virtually limited to Egyptian papyri"; γραμματεία "virtually restricted to Egyptian papyri"; εὐείλατος "well attested in the papyri but not elsewhere"; λαξευτήριον "well attested in Egyptian papyri"; μετανάστης "several times in Egyptian papyri." For further discussion see J. K. Aitken, "Jewish Worship amid Greeks: The Lexical Context of the Old Greek Psalter," in *The Temple in Text and Tradition* (ed. T. McLay; London: T. & T. Clark), forthcoming.

24. G. A. Deissmann, "Hellenistic Greek," in *The New Schaff–Herzog Encyclopedia of Religious Knowledge* (ed. S. M. Jackson; 12 vols.; New York: Funk and Wagnalls, 1908–12), 5: 211–15 (213).

25. G. A. Deissmann, *Bible Studies: Contributions, Chiefly from Papyri and Inscriptions, to the History of the Language, the Literature, and the Religion of Hellenistic Judaism and Primitive Christianity* (Edinburgh: T. & T. Clark, 1909), 91; cf. O. Montevecchi, "Quaedam de graecitate psalmorum cum papyris comparata," in *Bibbia e papiri. Luce dai papiri sulla Bibbia greca, a cura di A. Passoni Dell'Acqua* (Estudios de Papirologia y Filologia Biblica 5; Barcelona: Institut de Teologia fondamental, Seminari de papirologia, 1999), 97–120 (106).

to him in order to resolve a legal dispute.[26] What is striking about this word, and passed over by previous commentators, is that the word never appears in literary sources that are not Jewish or Christian.[27] Equally striking is the fact that it does not appear in inscriptions, apart from Christian ones. In this case, therefore, the inscriptions provide important counter-evidence. Since the word is only attested in papyri from Egypt, and not in documentary sources from elsewhere (primarily inscriptions), it suggests that this is a specifically Egyptian, or perhaps better Ptolemaic, word.

2. ἀρχισωματοφύλαξ

A straightforward example is ἀρχισωματοφύλαξ, a technical term for an official in the Ptolemaic court that is generally translated 'chief bodyguard,' although this does not reflect the function as an honorary title in the court. It is well attested in papyri from Egypt and appears to be specific to the Ptolemaic court, such that we might easily conclude that, when it appears in the Septuagint (1 Kgdms 28:2; Esth 2:21), it is an indication of an Egyptian location for the translators.[28] The appearance of the term in eight inscriptions from Cyprus, however, indicates that it was used in other locations too. The majority of these inscriptions are from the second century B.C.E. and reflect Ptolemaic court terminology, such as the altar dedication in Kition (modern Larnaka) to Zeus Soter and Athena Nikephoros on behalf of Ptolemy IX Soter II (late second century B.C.E.) and his children:

[Σω]τῆρος καὶ τῶν τέκνων αὐτοῦ οἱ ἐν Κιτίωι
[τα]σσόμενοι πρῶτοι φίλοι καὶ ἀρχισωματο-
[φύ]λακες καὶ ἡγεμόνες ἐπ᾽ ἀνδρῶν
[καὶ] περὶ τὸ σῶμα μαχαιροφόροι.[29]

The people [li]ned up in Kition, first friends and chief body[gu]ards and leaders of men [and] armed bodyguards of [So]ter and his children

Other examples, all from Cyprus, include in chronological order: *ArchPap* 13 (1939) 23, 11 (Lampousa, 193–186? B.C.E.), IKourion 43 (192–183 B.C.E.), IKition 2021 (164–145 B.C.E.), *ABSA* 56 (1961) 4, 4 (Kouklia, 163–145 B.C.E.), SEG 41:1478 (Kouklia, c. 154 B.C.E.), *ABSA* 56 (1961)

---

26. Including in addresses to Ptolemies as gods (UPZ 1.14.r2.18; 157 B.C.E.).

27. See J. K. Aitken, "Context of Situation in Biblical Lexica," in *Foundations for Syriac Lexicography III: Colloquia of the International Syriac Language Project* (ed. J. Dyk and W. van Peursen; Perspectives on Syriac Linguistics 4; Piscataway, NJ: Gorgias, 2008), 181–201 (195–96).

28. So Tov, "Reflections," 15.

29. *ArchPap* 13 (1939) 34, 16 (I.Kition 2003).

18, 46 (unspecified location and date), and *ABSA* 56 (1961) 20, 53 (unspecified location and date). It is of course no surprise to find these examples in Cyprus since the island was within the jurisdiction of the Ptolemaic kingdom. It was first taken by Ptolemy I in 311/310 B.C.E., and after being lost in 306 it was retaken in 294 to be ruled by a Ptolemaic *strategos* for the next two centuries.[30] These examples from Cyprus are, however, a reminder that anywhere in contact with the Ptolemies could have people with such titles, and we should be cautious of attributing the features to Egypt without question.

3. γαζοφύλαξ

Loanwords can be a helpful indicator of location, dependent upon where the donor language is distributed. The problem is that once a word has entered the language it can spread easily, especially if there is no suitable equivalent in the receptor language. A good example, though, is the word γαζοφύλαξ 'treasury keeper' and cognates, a formation of γάζα which is a derivative from Persian.[31] Since θησαυροφύλαξ already existed in Greek there was no particular requirement to use γαζοφύλαξ. Speakers of the language need not have been aware that γάζα was ultimately of Persian origin, but one can hypothesize that contact with the form γάζα or γαζοφύλαξ would have been more likely in regions formerly under Persian rule (which in the Hellenistic period particularly covered the Seleucid empire). In the Septuagint γαζοφύλαξ is found four times (1 Par [=1 Chr] 28:1; 1 Esd 2:10; 8:19; 8:45)[32] although γαζοφυλάκιον appears twenty-five times (especially in 1 Esdras, 2 Esdras, and 2 Maccabees). The synonymous θησαυροφύλαξ is only found once (2 Esd 5:14). If all the Septuagint has a provenance in Egypt, these results are slightly surprising when one considers the distribution of the terms in documentary sources.

In Egyptian papyri there is one occurrence of γαζοφύλαξ (P.Cair.Zen. 1.59036.4 [TM 696]; 257 B.C.E.) but it is in a letter from Apollodotos, who was based in Caria, and refers to the γαζοφύλαξ in Halicarnassus. Thus the one appearance in Egypt of the term is in reference to a person with that title in Asia Minor. There is nonetheless one appearance of the noun γάζα (P.Tebt. 3.1 739.22 [TM 5342]; 145 B.C.E.). This may be contrasted with nine examples of θησαυροφύλαξ between 300 and 50 B.C.E., and 277 examples of θησαυρός in the same time period. The inscriptions likewise

---

30. G. M. Cohen, *Hellenistic Settlements in Europe, the Islands and Asia Minor* (Hellenistic Culture and Society 17; Berkeley, CA: University of California Press, 1995), 35.

31. *EDG* 1: 254–55.

32. Z. Talshir, *I Esdras: A Text Critical Commentary* (SBLSCS 50; Atlanta, GA: Society of Biblical Literature, 2001), 101.

contain many examples of θησαυρός and cognates, but also a few more examples of γάζα and related compounds. There is one instance of γάζα in an inscription from Pergamon (after 133 B.C.E.) (ἐκ τῶν βασιλικῶν γα[ζῶν)[33] and one of γαζοφυλάκιον from Ionia.[34] There are also three instances of γαζοφύλαξ, but they are all from the Roman period and therefore of less relevance (though still important) for the later Septuagint translations.[35] They are still significant for their locations, in that two are found on the north shore of the Black Sea and the third in Dura-Europos on the Euphrates. The evidence overall, then, is very slight, but does favour the form γάζα and compounds appearing in Seleucid rather than Ptolemaic regions. No conclusions can be drawn on this evidence alone, especially given the translatability of terms across geographic regions, but it can be part of an argument should other evidence be available.

4. εὐ(ε)ίλατος

A more complex example is that of εὐ(ε)ίλατος. The adjective εὐ(ε)ίλατος 'merciful' (a derivative of ἵλημι) at one time seemed to be a distinctly biblical word. It serves as a synonym of ἵλαος, a frequent adjective in the Orphic hymns (e.g., 17b.9; 18.19).[36] The cognate verb εὐιλατεύω, presumably derived from the adjective, is still only attested in the Septuagint (Deut 29:19; Jdt 16:15; Ps 102[103]:3) and quotations from it, but the evidence that can now be compiled of the adjective would suggest that it is only the chance of survival that restricts the verb to the Septuagint. In the early days of papyri discoveries, upon coming across an example of εὐ(ε)ίλατος, Mahaffy was able to say that it "is known only in the LXX."[37] That we now have approximately forty attestations in papyri and inscriptions is indicative of the value that such material can bring.

In the Septuagint εὐ(ε)ίλατος is found in a Psalm as an equivalent of the Hebrew נֹשֵׂא:

κύριε ὁ θεὸς ἡμῶν, σὺ ἐπήκουες αὐτῶν·
ὁ θεός, σὺ εὐίλατος ἐγίνου αὐτοῖς
καὶ ἐκδικῶν ἐπὶ πάντα τὰ ἐπιτηδεύματα αὐτῶν. (Ps 98[99]:8)

---

33. MDAI(A) 33 (1908) 381, 3.9
34. OGIS 225.37 (253 B.C.E.) from Didyma.
35. CIRB 45.3 (93–124 C.E.); CIRB 49.9 (second century C.E.); SEG 2:824 (third century C.E.), with the spelling γαζοφ(ύλαξ).
36. So V. F. Vanderlip, *The Four Greek Hymns of Isidorus and the Cult of Isis* (American Studies in Papyrology 12; Toronto: Hakkert, 1972), 62.
37. J. P. Mahaffy, *The Flinders Petrie Papyri: With Transcriptions, Commentaries and Index* (3 vols.; Dublin: Academy House, 1893), 2: 46.

O Lord our God, you heard them;
O God, you were merciful to them,
although taking vengeance on all their devices.

It is also found in an apocryphal text in the context of prayer:

καὶ πάλιν ἐδεήθημεν τοῦ κυρίου ἡμῶν κατὰ ταῦτα καὶ εὐιλάτου
ἐτύχομεν. (1 Esd 8:53)

And we once more asked of our lord regarding these matters and we
happened to find him merciful.

Although εὐ(ε)ίλατος is attested in a few papyri, these are for the most part
in a non-religious context referring to royal favor. It is the inscriptions
primarily that provide us with religious examples of the word that corre-
spond to the use in the Septuagint, and it is the inscriptions that confirm
the word was used more widely than in Egypt alone. The papyri vary in
usage. The earliest example is from the Zenon archive (12th Feb, 257
B.C.E.), in which Zoilos advises Apollonios:

καλῶς οὖν ἔχει, Ἀπολλώνιε, ἐπακολουθῆσαί σε τοῖς ὑπὸ τοῦ θεοῦ
προστάγμασιν, ὅπως ἂν εὐίλατός σοι ὑπάρχων ὁ Σάραπις. (P.Cair.Zen.
1.59034.19 [TM 694])

It seemed fitting, therefore, Apollonios, that you heed the orders of
the god, so that Sarapis might be merciful to you

Although this is an equivalent example to the Septuagint ones, with reference to divine mercy, we find a year later a "secular" use pertaining to the
king (256–255 B.C.E.):

οὕτω γὰρ [ἔστα]ι τυχεῖν καὶ τὸν [ὕστερον χ]ρόνον εὐιλάτου τοῦ
βασιλ[έως. (P.Petr. 2.13 Fr19, l. 3 [TM 7634])

For thus [you will] find the ki[ng] even in [the fut]ure merciful

Other examples of royal 'favor' include a papyrus (PSI 4.392.6 [TM
2076]) from the year 242–241 B.C.E. and from Memphis in the first century B.C.E. (UPZ 1.109.6 [TM 3501]; 98 B.C.E.). The adjective is one of a
number of examples of words noted by Montevecchi from royal petition-
ary language applied to a god (as ἀντιλήμπτωρ). The Septuagint translator
has adopted a term of divine favor already in use since at least the mid-
third century B.C.E. As it derives from the Ptolemaic court, it might suggest an Egyptian setting for the translators. Such a hypothesis has to be
tested against the evidence of the inscriptions.

The most frequent occurrences of εὐ(ε)ίλατος are in the curse tablets from Knidos (second to first centuries B.C.E.). In these the petitioner

requests that the person, by whom she has been wronged, not find Demeter and Kore εὐ(ε)ίλατος, either if he does not confess, or in some cases
irrespective of whether he confesses or not.[38] For example:

> καὶ μὴ γένοιτο | εὐειλάτ[ου] τυ|χεῖν Δάματρο[ς], | ἀλλὰ μεγάλα|ς
> βασάνους βασ|ανιζομένα (IKnidos I 147 A.24)
>
> And may he not find Demet[er] propiti[ous], but that he be
> tormented by tumultuous torments

The expression in these texts is formulaic and repetitious, but regular in
its appeal to the minor deities Demeter and Kore. Citations through the
centuries in inscriptions from a variety of locations reveal that other cult
figures, like Demeter and Kore,[39] are often the ones who are sought out
as εὐ(ε)ίλατος: Sarapis (as above), Amonrasonter (Egypt, 131 B.C.E.: UPZ
2.199.8 [TM 3601]), Pan (Egypt, 20 C.E.: SB 5:8581.5[40]), Men Tyrannos
(Attica, first century C.E.: IG II² 1365.25; 1366.11, 26), or unspecified
"gods" (Maeonia, Asia Minor, first century C.E.: TAM V 1–2 167a.13).
Most striking of all is an occurrence in a hymn to Isis (IEgVers 175.25–
26 [TM 6304]), attributed in the inscription to one Isidorus and dated
c. 100–80 B.C.E.[41]

> Κλῦθι ἐμῶν εὐχῶν, μεγαλοσθενὲς οὔνομ᾽ ἔχουσ[α]
> εὐείλατος ἐμοί τε γείνου, λύπης μ᾽ ἀνάπαυσον ἁπάσης.
>
> Hear my prayers, you of the most powerful name, and be merciful to
> me, relieving me of all pain.

This is one of four hymns to Isis attributed to Isidorus and carved on the
walls of the temple of Isis in Narmunthis (Medinet Madi in the Fayum).
The hymnographer asks that the goddess be merciful (εὐείλατος), notably
using the same verb γίνομαι as Ps 98(99):8.

It is clear from the inscriptional evidence that the word was used in a
broad geographical spread across the Mediterranean, not just in Egypt but
in Asia Minor and as far away as Attica. Thus it is clearly not the case that
the word is exclusive to Egypt or that it could be used as an indication of an
Egyptian setting for a translation.[42] However, the evidence may be nuanced.

---

38. IKnidos I 147 A.24; 150A ll. 4, 9; 151 ll. 5, 10; 152A ll. 5, 8; 152B l. 7; 154 ll.
12, 14; 158A ll. 6, 8; 256A l. 24; 260 ll. 5, 10; 261 ll. 4, 9; 263 ll. 4, 6; 264 l. 6; 266 ll. 12,
13; 270 l. 6.

39. Demeter is also appealed to in a lead tablet from Amorgos, dated to the second
century C.E. See T. Homolle, "Inscriptions d'Amorgos: lames de plomb portant des imprecations," BCH 25 (1901): 412–56 (413–17).

40. A. Bernand, De Koptos à Kossier (Leiden: Brill, 1972), 43.

41. Text of Vanderlip, Four Greek Hymns.

42. A. Pietersma, "Place of Origin."

The examples suggest that the adjective is a shared epithet for a divinity in appeals and prayers, and that for the most part it is used in small cults rather than in reference to the gods of traditional Greek religion. Pleket suggests that the apparent use of the term only in minor religious cults (Sarapis, Isis, Demeter, Men) might account for its adoption by the Septuagint translators, to avoid a word with strong religious associations in Greek society.[43] If he is correct, then we have insight into the lexical choice by the translators, participating in a shared cultic vocabulary. But there is one further inscription to consider, from the most geographically distant source.

A first-century B.C.E. graffito from Roman Pompeii is noticeable for its location so far west in comparison to the examples so far considered:

- -] καὶ θεῶν | εὐειλάτων | Φιλάδελφος εὐχήν (SEG 30:1180)

This inscription is engraved in the interior of a black-glazed plate that probably formed part of a bowl which could have been transported here. This shows how easily vocabulary can travel, although in this case there may be more to it. As noted by the editor, "the name of the dedicant is characteristically, though not specifically, Egyptian" and the unnamed gods of the inscription are possibly Egyptian gods.[44] The graffito was found outside the Porta Nola probably during the excavations of the temple of Isis in 1765–66. De Caro therefore even proposes restoring the damaged opening as [Εἴσιδος] καὶ θεῶν . . . ,[45] confirming that the object might have been an offering to Isis and the other "favourable" gods. Despite the geographical distance the resonance of Egypt is still felt.

Returning to the list of gods requested to be εὐ(ε)ίλατος we notice how many are in fact characteristically Egyptian: Sarapis, Isis, Men, Amonrasonter. It is possible, therefore, that we do have in this case a word that was originally an Egyptian term, but soon came to be used more widely, if still primarily for Egyptian cults. Although it is not exclusively Egyptian, as demonstrated by its application to Demeter in Asia Minor, it still might have been more common in Egypt, and therefore it was adopted by the Septuagint translators. Pleket's suggestion that it was chosen to avoid other terms used in the main Greek cults seems unnecessary. To summarize, although εὐ(ε)ίλατος is not attested in literary sources,[46] it is frequent in documentary papyri (hence from Egypt) from the third

---

43. H. W. Pleket, "Religious History as the History of Mentality: The 'Believer' as Servant of the Deity in the Greek World," in *Faith, Hope and Worship: Aspects of Religious Mentality in the Ancient World* (ed. H. S. Versnel; Leiden: Brill, 1981), 152–92.

44. SEG 30:1180 (325).

45. S. De Caro, "Novità isiache dalla Campania," *La Parola del passato: rivista di studi antichi* 49 (1994): 7–21 (8).

46. Seneca's knowledge of the word in 54 C.E., in what appears to be an unidentified quotation, is striking (*divi claudii apocolocyntosis* 8.3 166): "*deus fieri vult: parum est*

century B.C.E. onwards referring to the king or a god. From the second
century B.C.E. it is found most often as a predicate of a god, both in Egypt
(e.g., Isis) and elsewhere of Egyptian gods, and in Asia Minor (Demeter).
Inscriptions show that the word was used over a much wider geographical
spread. However, from the evidence presented here, Pietersma still might
be correct that it is typical of Egypt, but it does not conclusively prove an
Egyptian setting for the Greek Psalms.

5. *παστοφόριον*

The noun παστοφόριον appears surprisingly frequently in the Septuagint: fourteen times in thirteen verses covering the translations of 1 and 2
Paralipomena, 1 Esdras, 1 Maccabees, Isaiah, Jeremiah, and Ezekiel. The
noun first appears in third-century B.C.E. papyri (e.g., P.Eleph. 20.17–18
[TM 5853]; Apollonopolites, 223–222 B.C.E.) and accordingly is marked
in LEH ("neol.?," 474). It does not appear at all in literature outside of
the Septuagint itself and works dependent upon it (Josephus; Eusebius)
so that its register is more documentary than literary. The meaning of
παστοφόριον is a chamber assigned to παστοφόροι (LSJ 1346), priests of a
certain class.[47] It is therefore chosen in the Septuagint as an appropriate
equivalent for the room in the Jerusalem temple. From its appearance
in 22 papyri between the third and first centuries B.C.E. it might appear
as a distinctly Egyptian term, used for the chamber of Egyptian priests.
In inscriptions there are seven appearances, all from the second century
B.C.E. and all from Delos.[48] This is another example of a term extending
beyond Egypt. However, in the majority of the Delian inscriptions, it is
in dedications to Isis, Sarapis, and Anoubis, and therefore for specifically

quod templum in Britannia habet, quod hunc barbari colunt et ut deum orant μωροῦ εὐϊλάτου
τυχεῖν?" Note the same use of the verb.

47. The interpretation of παστοφόρος is usually given (following LSJ 1346) as one ap-
pointed for carrying a παστός. LSJ takes παστός as possibly meaning a shrine (derivative of a
marriage chamber) and therefore proposes that a παστοφόρος was a priest who carried shrines
of the gods in procession. The root of παστός is the verb πάσσω 'to strew, sprinkle' and 'to
weave' (see *EDG* 1155) and it is therefore also possible that the παστοφόρος is one who bears
water libations, especially when it is interchangeable in P.Choach.Survey 17 with χοαχύτης.
It translates the Demotic *wn*, which has been interpreted as 'shrine opener' (CDD W: 89),
which would support the meaning 'shrine' but used in a different sense. However, E. N.
Lane, "Παστός," *Glotta* 66 (1988): 100–123, demonstrates how παστός always denotes a
piece of woven fabric, often associated with marriage, and never a shrine or a (bridal) chamber. Such an understanding arose from confusion with the etymologically unrelated παστάς.
For παστοφόροι he suggests (120–23) they were priests who carried such a woven fabric,
symbolic of the sacred marriage between Isis and Osiris, and of Isis as protector of marriage.

48. IDelos 1416 (156/5 B.C.E.), IDelos 1417 (155/4 B.C.E.), IDelos 1442 (146/5–
145/4 B.C.E. [partially reconstructed]), IDelos 1452 (after 145 B.C.E.), IDelos 2085 (112/1
B.C.E.), IDelos 2086 (112/1 B.C.E.), and IDelos 2124 (before 112/1 B.C.E.).

Egyptian cults. Since the Persian wars the island had been a focal point of the Delian League, which continued to function as the Island League under Ptolemaic protection. There was a close association with the Ptolemies upon whom the island was dependent,[49] paying cult honors to Soter (SIG 390; cf. Callimachus' *Hymn to Delos*), holding an annual Ptolemaia celebrating the island's association with the King (IG XI 4.1038), and dedicating statues to Ptolemy (OGIS 25).[50] This close connection with Egypt led to the early establishment of Egyptian cult sites on the island, and to the founding of two Sarapeia.[51]

The appearance of παστοφόριον in inscriptions, therefore, shows both the spread of a word beyond Egypt but at the same time its continuing association with Egyptian religion. The evidence does not prove an Egyptian origin for texts that use it, but renders it likely. If the word is associated with Egyptian cults, then it is all the more striking how it is used in the Septuagint.

6. ὑπομνηματογράφος

The noun ὑπομνηματογράφος is only attested from the Ptolemaic period on, almost exclusively in papyri and the Septuagint. In the Septuagint it translates the title מזכיר 'recorder' or 'secretary' in the royal court (1 Par [=1 Chr] 18:15; 2 Par [=2 Chr] 34:8; Isa 32:3, 22). The translation choice is fitting as a contemporary equivalent in the Ptolemaic court for an office in the Israelite monarchy. The definition given in LSJ is extensive and emphasizes the Egyptian context for the term:

> *recorder*, name of a great official in the Egyptian king's household, and the corresponding official in the office of the minister of finance (διοικητής), and prob. in those of other high officials. (LSJ 1889–90)

It is found in ten papyri between the third and first centuries B.C.E., and it becomes more frequent in the Roman period. Seeligman uses it as one of the examples of the translator's preference for Greek terms that were circulating in his Alexandrian milieu.[52] In this he follows LSJ in drawing attention to the Egyptian context for the word. It is certainly frequent in

---

49. Bagnall, *Administration*, 154.

50. R. L. Hunter, *Theocritus: Encomium of Ptolemy Philadelphus. Text and Translation with Introduction and Commentary* (Hellenistic Culture and Society 39; Berkeley, CA: University of California Press, 2003), 143.

51. Cf. the aretalogy to Sarapis (IG XI 4.1299).

52. I. L. Seeligman, *The Septuagint Version of Isaiah: A Discussion of Its Problems* (Mededelingen en verhandelingen van het Vooraziatisch-Egyptisch Genootschap "Ex Oriente Lux" 9; Leiden: Brill, 1948), 43.

Egyptian papyri and a few instances are found in Egyptian inscriptions, but four instances in inscriptions from Cyprus are of importance here. Three are in dedicatory inscriptions on a statue, and one is an honorific inscription for Ptolemy IX Alexander.[53] The title is clearly one for the Ptolemaic official governing Cyprus (see above, ἀρχισωματοφύλαξ, for Ptolemaic rule in Cyprus):

> . . . [. .]γαντην Λόχου το[ῦ] Κα<λ>[λιμήδου] | [τ]οῦ συγγενοῦς καὶ ὑπερμάχου | καὶ ὑπομνηματογράφου καὶ στρατηγοῦ | αὐτοκράτορος τῆς Θηβαΐδος (OGIS 147.1–4 [TM 6034])

> . . . [dau]ghter (?) of Lochos so[n] of Kal[limedes, t]he kinsman and defender and recorder and ruler-general of the Thebaid

OGIS 163 is an inscription for a statute dedicated to Aristonice and family. He was an honorary member of the Dionysiac Artists Guild and is praised for his services to the city of Paphos, 114–107 B.C.E. As an ὑπομνηματογράφος he too was one of the great royal officials. Ptolemaic connections always seem to lie behind this title.

Conclusion

It has been shown that it is very difficult to identify words as having a specific regional focus. Inscriptions provide evidence of a broad geographical spread and only in one case (ἀντιλήμπτωρ) where no inscriptions contain the word can we suggest an Egyptian provenance. This conclusion is always liable to be disproven by future epigraphic finds. In the other cases it was seen that the words are attested beyond the confines of Egypt, and therefore cannot be used to demonstrate an Egyptian origin for particular Septuagint books. However, in apparent contradiction, some of these were found outside Egypt only in major Ptolemaic possessions, suggesting they were particular to the vocabulary of the Ptolemaic administration. Some too were found particularly in the context of Egyptian cults abroad, which would also imply an Egyptian origin for the words. The conclusions can only be tentative but the data indicate some words could have a regional connection, even if that region should perhaps be defined in terms of administrative districts rather than countries. Words carry passports permitting them leave to travel.

---

53. Statue dedications (see T. B. Mitford, "The Hellenistic Inscriptions of Old Paphos," *ABSA* 56 [1961]: 1–41): *ABSA* 56 (1961): 29, 76 (= TM 6034; OGIS 147; SEG 13:575; 127–124 B.C.E.), *ABSA* 56 (1961): 35, 95 (OGIS 163; 114–107 B.C.E.), and *ABSA* 56 (1961): 28, 75 (127–124 B.C.E.; reconstructed on the basis of similar wording). Honorific inscription: SEG 25:1102 (114–107 B.C.E., ὑπομ[νηματογράφος).

Conclusions

This study has only been a beginning; over time more words will be identified, new discoveries published, inscriptions redated, readings disputed, and semantic contexts modified and reinterpreted. The lexicographic task is never at an end. Even identifying a word in an inscription is not a panacea. Once identified, a word and the inscription in which it resides still require examination and discussion, and, as all exegesis, that is an ongoing task. Some of my evidence will be shown by subsequent publication to be overturned or require significant reassessment, while some will find further support in new discoveries. Whatever reconsideration is made, it will be a sign that the book has been successful. The worst would be that no changes are proposed by future scholars, for that would mean that no one has taken up the challenge of incorporating epigraphic material into their research.

In many ways the words I have chosen are the obscure or the rare, covering titles, animals, and material objects. Much more work would be required to examine standard verbs, such as καθίστημι or πορεύομαι, and thus to reshape the semantic presentations of lexicons. This is certainly required, but will take time. The task here has been to show that there are resources available for undertaking such a mammoth enterprise, and that the fruits may well be worthwhile. Certainly, the omission of inscriptions from scholarly discussions has been common, and their full value will only be appreciated once they have been sufficiently included. This book has already made this point, but some brief concluding reflections on the wider consequences of this topic are in order.

1. Future lexicons

Although some weaknesses have been noted in Septuagint lexicons, the field is in a far stronger position than ever before. GELS coupled with LEH now offer a complete analysis of the Septuagint words in context, and the semantic analysis by Muraoka should form the basis of all future work. This means that there is no immediate need for another lexicon. It does not, however, entail abandoning any further work in this area.

Rather, it signifies that any future lexicon will only be an advance if it takes into consideration the full range of data. The future lies in expanding the lexicons to include the history of each word in the language, with particular focus on its place in contemporary Greek. It was one of the principles of the *Oxford English Dictionary* that words have lives and that lexicographers should trace their biographies. In the words of H. Coleridge, the first editor: "Every word should be made to tell its own story—the story of its birth and life, and in many cases of its death, and even occasionally of its resuscitation."[1] A systematic analysis of the Septuagint in the light of papyri, inscriptions, and literary sources of the Hellenistic and Roman periods would be a major undertaking, but is the only way to advance.

2. Septuagint Greek

Examination of the inscriptions shows the range of genres and registers from which Septuagint vocabulary derives. Political treaties, sacred laws, poetic epitaphs, and religious hymns all contain parallels to the Greek vocabulary used by the translators. No easy conclusion can be drawn from this, but it demonstrates the variety within the Septuagint. It also shows how difficult questions need to be asked about register and connotation of words, and that the inscriptions offer some useful material for further reflection. Although Deissmann's focus on "popular" Greek has been shown to be an insufficient label, its influence can still be felt in some circles. The contemporary Greek of the Septuagint is elucidated from a range of sources and registers. It is this eclectic nature of the language that does not permit simple sociological descriptions of the translators or their language. Scholars must take into account both the translation technique and the varied literary nature of the Greek to appreciate fully the language of the translators.[2]

3. Septuagint studies

Language study should form the basis of Septuagint studies. In discovering the use of words in the manner shown here—the contexts in which they are used, the religious or social associations, the literary register, or their precise meanings—the message being conveyed by the transla-

---

1. H. Coleridge, "A Letter to The Very Rev. The Dean of Westminster from Herbert Coleridge, Esq.," *Transactions of the Philological Society* 4 (1857): 71–78 (72).

2. For discussion of these issues, see J. K. Aitken, "The Language of the Septuagint and Jewish Greek Identity," in *The Jewish–Greek Tradition in Antiquity and the Byzantine Empire* (ed. J. K. Aitken and J. Carleton Paget; Cambridge: Cambridge University Press, 2014), 120–34.

tors is revealed. Appreciation of the translation technique and of the selection of words by the translators can only happen once the meanings and connotations of the words are known. Likewise, the translators's choices that might reveal exegetical or theological decisions can be determined only once the full biographies of the words are understood. The vocabulary sheds light on the educational levels, literary sensibilities, and social interactions of the silent individuals behind the texts. It is therefore not merely an interest of the few scholars engaged in lexicography, but should be fundamental for all in the field.

Appendix:
Epigraphic Resources

Handbooks

McLean, B. H., *An Introduction to Greek Epigraphy of the Late Hellenistic and Roman Periods from Alexander the Great down to the Reign of Constantine (323 B.C.–A.D. 337)* (Ann Arbor: University of Michigan Press, 2002). — Most recent and helpful guide to inscriptions from this period.

Cook, B. F., *Greek Inscriptions* (London: British Museum, 1987). — Examples of inscriptions, with a short bibliography.

Jeffery, L. H., *The Local Scripts of Archaic Greece* (revised edition; Oxford: Clarendon, 1990). — Corpus of early Greek inscriptions, with illustrations and comments. First edition, 1961.

Woodhead, A. G., *A Study of Greek Inscriptions* (2nd edition; Cambridge: Cambridge University Press, 1981). — A standard in the field, if now dated.

Guarducci, M., *Epigrafia Greca* (4 volumes; Rome: Istituto poligrafico dello Stato, 1967–78). — Large and complete handbook in Italian.

Bodel, J., *Epigraphic Evidence: Ancient History From Inscriptions* (Approaching the Ancient World; London: Routledge, 2001). — Guide to using inscriptions in historical reconstruction.

Cooper, C. R. *Epigraphy and the Greek Historian* (PhoenixSup 47; Toronto: University of Toronto Press, 2008). — Guide to using inscriptions in historical reconstruction.

Reference tools

Bulletin Epigraphique
A yearly review of publications and finds by J. and L. Robert. After the death of L. Robert, Ph. Gauthier started a new series (1987–).

Supplementum Epigraphicum Graecum (Leiden: Brill).
A comprehensive summary of publications in the field. Online for those with an institutional subscription.

Epigraphic Bulletin for Greek Religion
The EBGR appears in the journal *Kernos* (Online: www.kernos.ulg.ac.be) and records new epigraphic finds relating to Greek religion. Concise indexes can be found on the website.

Internet resources

Packhum Inscriptions
The main freely accessible database for inscriptions: epigraphy.packhum.org/inscriptions/

Papyri.info
The main freely accessible database for papyri, incorporating a number of resources: papyri.info

IG online
The IG volumes, with German translations (more to be added in the future): telota.bbaw.de/ig/

CLAROS Concordance of Greek inscriptions
A database of epigraphic volumes: www.dge.filol.csic.es/claros/cnc/2cnc.htm

Current Epigraphy Blog
A regular roundup of news in the field: www.currentepigraphy.org/

Bibliography

F. Bérard, D. Feissel, N. Laubry, P. Petitmengin, D. Rousset, M. Sève et collaborateurs, *Guide de l'épigraphiste: Bibliographie choisie des épigraphies antiques et médiévales* (4th edition; Guides et inventaires bibliographiques de la Bibliothèque de l'École normale supérieure 7; Paris: Rue d'Ulm, 2010). — This is the latest bibliographic guide. It is a hard copy publication, but supplements are available online: www.antiquite.ens.fr/ressources/publications-aux-p-e-n-s/guide-de-l-epigraphiste/article/overview

Bibliography

Adams, S. A., "Review of J. Cook and A. van der Kooij, *Law, Prophets, and Wisdom: On the Provenance of Translators and Their Books in the Septuagint Version* (CBET 68; Leuven: Peeters, 2012," *RBL* 08/2013 [online:www.bookreviews.org] (2013).

Adrados, F. R., "Léxico de inscripciones y dialectal," in *Introducción a la lexicografía griega* (ed. F. R. Adrados, E. Gangutia, J. López Facal, and C. Serrano Aybar; Madrid: CSIC, 1977), 169–83.

Adrados, F. R., ed., *Diccionario Griego-Español, por E. Gangutia, L. Facal, C. Serrano, P. Bádenas y otros colaboradores* (Madrid: Instituto Antonio de Nebrija, 1980–).

Aitken, J. K., "Context of Situation in Biblical Lexica," in *Foundations for Syriac Lexicography III: Colloquia of the International Syriac Language Project* (ed. J. Dyk and W. van Peursen; Perspectives on Syriac Linguistics 4; Piscataway, NJ: Gorgias, 2008), 181–201.

———, "Jewish Worship amid Greeks: The Lexical Context of the Old Greek Psalter," in *The Temple in Text and Tradition* (ed. T. McLay; London: T. & T. Clark), forthcoming.

———, "The Language of the Septuagint and Jewish Greek Identity," in *The Jewish–Greek Tradition in Antiquity and the Byzantine Empire* (ed. J. K. Aitken and J. Carleton Paget; Cambridge: Cambridge University Press, 2014), 120–34.

———, "The Language of the Septuagint: Recent Theories, Future Prospects," *BJGS* 24 (1999): 24–33.

———, "The Literary Attainment of the Translator of Greek Sirach," in *The Texts and Versions of the Book of Ben Sira: Transmission and Interpretation* (ed. J.-S. Rey and J. Joosten; Leiden: Brill, 2011), 95–126.

———, "Neologisms: A Septuagint Problem," in *Interested Readers: Essays on the Hebrew Bible in Honor of David J. A. Clines* (ed. J. K. Aitken, J. M. S. Clines, and C. M. Maier; Atlanta: SBL, 2013), 315–29.

_____ , "Phonological Phenomena in Greek Papyri and Inscriptions and Their Significance for the Septuagint," in *Studies in the Greek Bible: Essays in Honor of Francis T. Gignac, S.J.* (ed. J. Corley and V. Skemp; CBQMS 44; Washington, D.C.: The Catholic Biblical Association of America, 2008), 256–77.

_____ , "Rhetoric and Poetry in Greek Ecclesiastes," *BIOSCS* 38 (2005): 55–78.

_____ , "Σχοῖνος in the Septuagint," *VT* 50 (2000): 433–44.

Allen, W. C., "On the Meaning of ΠΡΟΣΗΛΥΤΟΣ in the Septuagint," *Expositor* 4.10 (1894): 264–75.

Arzt-Grabner, P., and C. M. Kreinecker, eds., *Light from the East: Papyrologische Kommentare zum Neuen Testament: Akten des internationalen Symposions vom 3.–4. Dezember 2009 am Fachbereich Bibelwissenschaft und Kirchengeschichte der Universität Salzburg* (Wiesbaden: Harrassowitz, 2010).

Austin, M. M., *The Hellenistic World from Alexander to the Roman Conquest: A Selection of Ancient Sources in Translation* (2nd ed.; Cambridge: Cambridge University Press, 2006).

Bagnall, R. S., *Everyday Writing in the Graeco-Roman East* (Sather Classical Lectures 69; Berkeley, CA: University of California Press, 2011).

_____ , *The Administration of the Ptolemaic Possessions outside Egypt* (Columbia Studies in the Classical Tradition 4; Leiden: Brill, 1976).

Bagnall, R. S., and P. Derow, *The Hellenistic Period: Historical Sources in Translation* (Blackwell Sourcebooks in Ancient History 1; Oxford: Blackwell, 2004).

Barr, J., "Words for Love in Biblical Greek," in *The Glory of Christ in the New Testament: Studies in Christology in Memory of George Bradford Caird* (ed. L. D. Hurst and N. T. Wright; Oxford: Clarendon, 1987), 3–18.

_____ , *The Semantics of Biblical Language* (London: Oxford University Press, 1961).

Bazzana, G. B., "New Testament Studies and Documentary Papyri: Interactions and New Perspectives," *Papyrologica Lupiensia* 22 (2013): 5–34.

Beekes, R., *Etymological Dictionary of Greek, with the Assistance of Lucien van Beek* (2 vols.; Leiden Indo-European Etymological Dictionary Series 10/1–2; Leiden: Brill, 2010).

Berichtigungsliste der griechischen Papyrusurkunden aus Ägypten (Berlin: Vereinigung Wissenschaftlicher Verleger, 1922–).

Bernand, A., *De Koptos à Kossier* (Leiden: Brill, 1972).

Bernand, E., *Inscriptions métriques de l'Égypte gréco-romaine: recherches sur la poésie épigrammatique des grecs en Égypte* (Annales littéraires de l'Université de Besançon 98; Paris: Belles lettres, 1969).

Bickerman, E. J., "The Septuagint as a Translation," *PAAJR* 28 (1959): 1–39.

Biel, J. C., *Novus Thesaurus Philologicus, sive lexicon in LXX et alios interpretes et scriptores apocryphos Veteris Testamenti* (3 vols.; Den Haag: Bouvink, 1779–81).

Boffo, L., *Iscrizioni greche e latine per lo studio della Bibbia* (Biblioteca di storia e storiografia dei tempi biblici 9; Brescia: Paideia, 1994).

Bons, E., and A. Passoni Dell'Acqua, "A Sample Article: κτίζω – κτίσις – κτίσμα – κτίστης," in *Septuagint Vocabulary: Pre-History, Usage, Reception* (ed. E. Bons and J. Joosten; SBLSCS 58; Atlanta: SBL, 2011), 173–88.

Bousquet, J., "Inscriptions de Delphes," *BCH* 88 (1964): 380–94.

Brockelmann, C., *Grundriss der vergleichenden Grammatik der semitischen Sprachen* (2 vols.; Berlin: Reuther & Reichard, 1908–13).

Bubeník, V., *Hellenistic and Roman Greece as a Sociolinguistic Area* (Amsterdam Studies in the Theory and History of Linguistic Science 4; Current Issues in Linguistic Theory 57; Amsterdam: Benjamins, 1989).

Buitenwerf, R., *Book III of the Sibylline Oracles and Its Social Setting, with an Introduction, Translation and Commentary* (Studia in Veteris Testamenti pseudepigrapha 17; Leiden: Brill, 2003).

Buraselis, K., M. Stefanou, and D. J. Thompson, eds., *The Ptolemies, the Sea and the Nile: Studies in Waterborne Power* (Cambridge: Cambridge University Press, 2013).

Burstein, S., *The Hellenistic Age From the Battle of Ipsos to the Death of Kleopatra VII* (Translated Documents of Greece and Rome 3; Cambridge: Cambridge University Press, 1985).

Cadell, H., "Vocabulaire de la législation ptolémaïque. Problème du sens de *dikaiôma* dans le Pentateuque," in Κατὰ τοὺς Ο΄. *"Selon les Septante": Trente études sur la Bible grecque des Septante. En hommage à Marguerite Harl* (ed. G. Dorival and O. Munnich; Paris: Cerf, 1995), 207–21.

Cagnat, R. et al., *Inscriptiones Graecae ad res Romanas pertinentes*, IV (Paris: Leroux, 1927).

Caird, G. B., "Towards a Lexicon of the Septuagint, I, II," *JTS* 19 (1968): 453–75; 20 (1969): 21–40.

Canali De Rossi, F., *Filius Publicus: Huios tês poleos e titoli affini in iscrizioni greche di età imperial. Studi sul vocabulario dell'evergesia* 1 (Rome: Herder, 2007).

Carson, D. A., *Exegetical Fallacies* (2nd ed.; Grand Rapids, MI: Baker, 1996).

Cavalier, C., *Esther* (La Bible d'Alexandrie 12; Paris: Cerf, 2012).

Chadwick, J., "The Case for Replacing Liddell and Scott," *BICS* 39 (1994): 1–11.

――――, *Lexicographica graeca: Contributions to the Lexicography of Ancient Greek* (Oxford: Clarendon, 1996).

Chaniotis, A., *Die Verträge zwischen kretischen Poleis in der hellenistischen Zeit* (Stuttgart: Steiner, 1996).

Chantraine, P., *La Formation des noms en grec ancient* (Paris: Champion, 1933), 379.

Chiricat, É., "Funérailles publiques et enterrement au gymnase à l' époque hellénistique," in *Citoyenneté et participation à la basse époque hellénistique* (ed. P. Fröhlich and C. Müller; Hautes Etudes du monde gréco-romain 35; Geneva: Droz, 2005), 214–22.

Clarysse, W., "Ethnic Diversity and Dialect among the Greeks of Hellenistic Egypt," in *The Two Faces of Graeco-Roman Egypt. Greek and Demotic and Greek–Demotic Texts and Studies Presented to P. W. Pestman* (ed. A. M. F. W. Verhoogt and S. P. Vleeming; Papyrologica Lugduno-Batava 30; Leiden: Brill, 1998), 1–13.

Clay, D., *Archilochos Heros: The Cult of Poets in the Greek Polis* (Hellenic Studies 6; Cambridge, MA: Harvard University Press, 2004).

Cohen, G. M., *Hellenistic Settlements in Europe, the Islands and Asia Minor* (Hellenistic Culture and Society 17; Berkeley, CA: University of California Press, 1995).

Coleridge, H., "A Letter to The Very Rev. The Dean of Westminster from Herbert Coleridge, Esq.," *Transactions of the Philological Society* 4 (1857): 71–78.

Colvin, S., "The Language of Non-Athenians in Old Comedy," in *The Rivals of Aristophanes* (ed. D. Harvey and J. Wilkins; London: Duckworth, 2000), 285–98.

Cook, B. F., *Greek Inscriptions* (Reading the Past; London: British Museum Publications for the Trustees of the British Museum, 1987).

Cook, J., *The Septuagint of Proverbs: Jewish and/or Hellenistic Proverbs? Concerning the Hellenistic Colouring of LXX Proverbs* (VTSup 69; Leiden: Brill, 1997).

Cook, J., and A. van der Kooij, *Law, Prophets, and Wisdom: On the Provenance of Translators and Their Books in the Septuagint Version* (CBET 68; Leuven: Peeters, 2012).

Cotton, H. M., and A. Yardeni, *Discoveries in the Judaean Desert: Volume XXVII. Aramaic, Hebrew and Greek Documentary Texts from Naḥal Ḥever and Other Sites* (Oxford: Clarendon, 1997).

Cunningham, I. C., *Synagoge:* Συναγωγὴ λέξεων χρησίμων (SGLG 10; Berlin: de Gruyter, 2003).

Danker, F. W., *A Greek–English Lexicon of the New Testament and Other Early Christian Literature* (3rd ed.; Chicago: University of Chicago Press, 2001).

Davies, E. W., *Numbers* (NCBC; Grand Rapids, MI: Eerdmans, 1995), 186–87.

De Caro, S., "Novità isiache dalla Campania," *La Parola del passato: rivista di studi antichi* 49 (1994): 7–21.

De Crom, D., "The Lexicon of LXX Canticles and Greco-Roman Papyri," *ZAW* 124 (2012): 255–62.

Debel, H., and E. Verbeke, "The Greek Rendering of Hebrew Hapax Legomena in the Book of Qoheleth," in *XIV Congress of the International Organization for Septuagint and Cognate Studies, Helsinki, 2010* (ed. M. K. H. Peters; Atlanta: Society of Biblical Literature, 2013), 313–31.

Deissmann, G. A., *Bibelstudien* (Marburg: Elwert, 1895).

_____ , *Bible Studies: Contributions, Chiefly from Papyri and Inscriptions, to the History of the Language, the Literature, and the Religion of Hellenistic Judaism and Primitive Christianity* (Edinburgh: T. & T. Clark, 1909).

_____ , "Hellenistic Greek," in *The New Schaff–Herzog Encyclopedia of Religious Knowledge* (ed. S. M. Jackson; 12 vols.; New York: Funk and Wagnalls, 1908–12), 5: 211–15.

_____ , "Hellenistic Greek with Special Consideration of the Greek Bible," in *The Language of the New Testament: Classic Essays* (ed. S. Porter; Sheffield: JSOT, 1991), 39–59.

_____ , "Hellenistisches Griechisch," in *Realencyklopädie für protestantische Theologie und Kirche* (ed. A. Hauk; 24 vols.; 3rd ed.; Leipzig: Hinrich, 1896–1913), 7: 627–39.

_____ , *Neue Bibelstudien* (Marburg: Elwert, 1897).

Denniston, J. D., *The Greek Particles* (2nd ed.; Oxford: Clarendon, 1954).

Dhorme, E., *A Commentary on the Book of Job. Translated by Harold Knight, with a Prefatory Note by H. H. Rowley* (London: Thomas Nelson, 1967).

Donderer, M., *Die Architekten der späten römischen Republik und der Kaiserzeit: Epigraphische Zeugnisse* (Erlanger Forschungen A: Geisteswissenschaften 69; Erlangen: Universitätsbibliothek Erlangen–Nürnberg, 1996).

Dorandi, T., "Korrekturzeichen," in *Der neue Pauly: Enzyklopädie der Antike* (16 vols.; ed. H. Cancik and H. Schneider; Stuttgart: Metzler, 1996–2003), 6: 759–60.

Driver, G. R., "Problems in the Hebrew Text of Job," *Wisdom in Israel and in the Ancient Near East* (ed. M. Noth and D. Winton Thomas; VTSup 3; Leiden: Brill, 1960), 72–93.

Ennabli, L., *Les inscriptions funéraires chrétiennes de Carthage. 2, La basilique de Mcidfa* (Collection de l'École française de Rome 62; Roma: École française de Rome, 1982).

Evans, T. V., "Complaints of the Natives in a Greek Dress: The Zenon Archive and the Problem of Egyptian Interference," in *Multilingualism in the Graeco-Roman Worlds* (ed. A. Mullen and P. James; Cambridge: Cambridge University Press, 2012), 106–23.

———, "A Note on βουλή in P.Col.Zen. I 10," *ZPE* 145 (2003): 246–48.

———, "Standard Koine Greek in Third Century BC Papyri," in *Proceedings of the Twenty-Fifth International Congress of Papyrology, Ann Arbor 2007* (ed. T. Gagos; Ann Arbor, MI: University of Michigan Press, 2010), 211–20.

———, "The Use of Linguistic Criteria for Dating Septuagint Books," *BIOSCS* 43 (2010): 5–22.

———, *Verbal Syntax in the Greek Pentateuch: Natural Greek Usage and Hebrew Interference* (Oxford: Oxford University Press, 2001).

Evans, T. V., and D. D. Obbink, "Introduction," in *The Language of the Papyri* (ed. T. V. Evans and D. D. Obbink; Oxford: Oxford University Press, 2009), 1–12.

Ewing, G., *A Greek Grammar, and Greek and English Scripture Lexicon Containing all the Words which Occur in the Septuagint and Apocrypha, as well as in the New Testament* (2nd ed.; Glasgow: J. Hedderwick for A. Constable, 1812).

Facal, J. L., "Historia de la lexicografía griega moderna," in *Introducción a la lexicografía griega* (F. R. Adrados, E. Gangutia, J. López Facal, and C. Serrano Aybar; Madrid: CSIC, 1977), 107–42.

Feldman, L. H., *Judean Antiquities 1–4: Translation and Commentary* (Leiden: Brill, 2004).

Ferguson, W. D., *The Legal Terms Common to the Macedonian Greek Inscriptions and the New Testament* (Chicago: University of Chicago, 1913).

Fernández Marcos, N., *The Septuagint in Context: Introduction to the Greek Versions of the Bible* (Leiden: Brill, 2000).

Flashar, M., "Exegetische Studien zum Septuagintapsalter," *ZAW* 32 (1912): 81–116, 161–89, 241–68.

Fraser, P. M., "Bibliography: Graeco-Roman Egypt: Greek Inscriptions (1956)," *JEA* 43 (1957): 101–9.

_____, "Bibliography: Graeco-Roman Egypt: Greek Inscriptions (1957)," *JEA* 44 (1958): 108–16.

Gabba, E., *Iscrizioni greche e latine per lo studio della Bibbia* (Sintesi dell'oriente e della Bibbia 3; Rome: Marietti, 1958).

Gager, J. G., *Curse Tablets and Binding Spells from the Ancient World* (Oxford: Oxford University Press, 1992).

Gallavotti, C., "La Stele di Ammonio," *La Parola del Passato* 12 (1957): 375–77.

_____, "Postilla alla nuova epigrafe alessandrina," in Ἀντίδωρον *Hugoni Henrico Paoli oblatum: Miscellanea philological* (Pubblicazioni, dell'Istituto di filologia classica 8; Genoa: Istituto di filologia classica, 1956), 323–24.

Gamble, H. T., *Books and Readers in the Early Church: A History of Early Christian Texts* (New Haven: Yale University Press, 1995), 13–14.

Gentry, P. J., *The Asterisked Materials in the Greek Job* (SBLSCS 38; Atlanta: Scholars, 1995).

Georgakopoulou, A., and M. S. Silk, eds., *Standard Languages and Language Standards: Greek, Past and Present* (Farnham: Ashgate, 2009).

Gerber, A., *Deissmann the Philologist* (BZNW 171; Berlin: de Gruyter, 2010).

Gerhard, G. A., *Charētos gnōmai* (Heidelberg: Winter, 1912).

Gosling, F. A., "The Inaccessible Lexicon of J. F. Schleusner," *JNSL* 26 (2000): 19–31.

Grainger, J. D., *The League of the Aitolians* (Mnemosyne, bibliotheca classica Batava. Supplementum 200; Leiden: Brill, 1999).

Grandjean, Y., *Une nouvelle Arétalogie d'Isis à Maronée* (Études préliminaires aux religions orientales dans l'Empire romain 49; Leiden: Brill, 1975).

Gray, J., *The Book of Job* (ed. D. J. A. Clines; The Text of the Hebrew Bible 1; Sheffield: Sheffield Phoenix, 2010).

Grelot, P., "Études sur les textes araméens d'Éléphantine," *RB* 78 (1971): 515–44.

Grenfell, B. P., *An Alexandrian Erotic Fragment and Other Greek Papyri Chiefly Ptolemaic* (Oxford: Clarendon, 1896).

———, ed., *Revenue Laws of Ptolemy Philadelphus* (Oxford: Clarendon, 1896).

Grenfell, B. P., and A. S. Hunt, *The Oxyrhynchus Papyri, Part XIV* (London: Egypt Exploration Society, 1920).

Groningen, B. A. van, "Projet d'unification des systèmes de signes critiques," *ChrEg* 7 (1932): 262–69.

Gwynn, R. M., "Notes on the Vocabulary of Ecclesiastes in Greek," *Hermathena* 42 (1920): 115–22.

Habel, N. C., *The Book of Job: A Commentary* (Philadelphia: Westminster, 1985), 157.

Hanhart, R., *Esther: Vetus Testamentum graecum auctoritate Academiae Scientiarum Gottingensis editum* (Göttingen: Vandenhoeck and Ruprecht, 1966).

Hauspie, K., "The LXX Quotations in the LSJ Supplements of 1968 and 1996," in *Biblical Greek Language and Lexicography: Essays in Honor of Frederick W. Danker* (ed. B. Taylor, J. Lee, P. Burton, and R. Whitaker; Grand Rapids, MI: Eerdmans, 2004), 108–25.

———, "Neologisms in the Septuagint of Ezekiel," *JNSL* 27 (2001): 17–37.

Heberdey, R., "Vorläufige Berichte über die Ausgrabungen in Ephesus," *JÖAI* 1 Beiblatt (1898): 54–82.

Heever, G. van den, "Redescribing Graeco-Roman Antiquity: On Religion and History of Religion," *Religion and Theology* 12 (2005): 211–38.

Heinen, H., "Zur Terminologie der Sklaverei im ptolemäischen Ägypten: παῖς und παιδίσκη in den Papyri und der Septuaginta," in *Atti del XVII Congresso internazionale di papirologia* (3 vols.; Naples: Centro Internazionale per lo Studio dei Papiri Ercolanesi, 1984), 3: 1287–95.

Heisserer, A. J., "IG XII, 2, 1 (The Monetary Pact between Mytilene and Phokaia)," *ZPE* 55 (1984): 115–32.

———, "Observations on 'IG' XII 2, 10 and 11," *ZPE* 74 (1988): 111–32.

Helly, B., *Gonnoi* (2 vols.; Amsterdam: Hakkert, 1973).

Hemmerdinger, B., "Noms communs grecs d'origine égyptienne," *Glotta* 46 (1968): 238–47.

Hernández Lara, C., "Rhetorical Aspects of Chariton of Aphrodisias," *Giornale Italiano di Filologia* 42 (1990): 267–74.

Herrmann, P., "Epigraphische Notizen: 18. ἱματιοφυλάκιον. 19. Stiftung des M. Feridius P. f. 20. Fragment einer Gladiatoreninschrift," *EA* 31 (1999): 31–34.

Herrmann, P., and K. Z. Polatkan, *Das Testament des Epikrates und andere neue Inschriften aus dem Museum von Manisa* (Vienna: Hermann Böhlaus Nachfolger, 1969).

Hiebert, R. J. V., "Lexicography and the Translation of a Translation: The NETS Version and the Septuagint of Genesis," *BIOSCS* 37 (2004): 73–86.

Hiller von Gaertringen, F., *Inscriptiones Graecae. Inscriptiones Atticae Euclidis anno anteriores, editio minor* (Berlin: de Gruyter, 1924).

Hodot, R., "Décret de Kymè en l'honneur du prytane Kléanax", *J. Paul Getty Museum Journal* 10 (1982): 165–80.

———, "Le décret de Kymè en l'honneur de Labéon," *ZPE* 19 (1975): 121–33.

Hodot, R., "Notes critiques sur le corpus épigraphique de Lesbos," *Etudes d'Archéologie classique* 5 (1976): 17–81.

Hoftijzer, J., and K. Jongeling, *Dictionary of the North-West Semitic Inscriptions* (2 vols.; HO 21; Leiden: Brill, 1995).

Hogeterp, A. L. A., "New Testament Greek as Popular Speech: Adolf Deissmann in Retrospect: A Case Study in Luke's Greek," *ZNW* 102 (2011): 178–200.

Holland, L. B., F. W. Householder, and R. L. Scranton, *A Sylloge of Greek Building Inscriptions* (unpublished manuscript, ASCS library, Athens).

Homolle, T., "Inscriptions d'Amorgos: lames de plomb portant des imprecations," *BCH* 25 (1901): 412–56.

Hornblower, S., *Mausolus* (Oxford: Clarendon, 1982).

Horsley, G. H. R., "Epigraphical Grammars," in *New Documents Illustrating Early Christianity, Volume 4: A Review of Greek Inscriptions and Papyri Published in 1979* (North Ryde, Australia: Ancient History Documentary Research Centre, Macquarie University, 1987), 273.

———, "Epigraphy as an Ancilla to the Study of the Greek Bible: A Propos of a Recent Anthology of Inscriptions," *Bib* 79 (1998): 258–67.

———, "The Fiction of 'Jewish Greek,'" in *New Documents Illustrating Early Christianity, Volume 5: Linguistic Essays* (North Ryde, Australia: Ancient History Documentary Research Centre, Macquarie University, 1989), 5–40.

_____ , "The Greek Documentary Evidence and NT Lexical Study: Some Soundings," in *New Documents Illustrating Early Christianity, Volume 5: Linguistic Essays* (North Ryde, Australia: Ancient History Documentary Research Centre, Macquarie University, 1989), 67–94.

_____ , "Koine or Atticism—A Misleading Dichotomy," in *New Documents Illustrating Early Christianity, Volume 5: Linguistic Essays* (North Ryde, Australia: Ancient History Documentary Research Centre, Macquarie University, 1989), 41–48.

_____ , "The Origin and Scope of Moulton and Milligan's Vocabulary of the Greek Testament, and Deissmann's Planned New Testament Lexicon. Some Unpublished Letters of G. A. Deissmann to J. H. Moulton," *BJRL* 76 (1994): 187–216.

_____ , "Res Bibliographicae: Divergent Views on the Nature of the Greek of the Bible," *Bib* 65 (1984): 393–403.

Horsley, G. H. R., and J. A. L. Lee, "A Preliminary Checklist of Abbreviations of Greek Epigraphic Volumes," *Epigraphica* 56 (1994): 129–69.

Hünemörder, C., "Giraffe," *Der Neue Pauly: Enzyklopädie der Antike* (ed. H. Cancik, H. Schneider, and M. Landfester; 16 vols.; Stuttgart: Metzler, 1996–2003), 4: 1075.

Hunter, R. L., *Theocritus: Encomium of Ptolemy Philadelphus. Text and Translation with Introduction and Commentary* (Hellenistic Culture and Society 39; Berkeley, CA: University of California Press, 2003).

Jacob, B., "Das Buch Esther bei den LXX," *ZAW* 10 (1890): 280–90.

Jacobson, D. M., *The Hellenistic Paintings of Marisa* (Palestine Exploration Fund Annual 7; Leeds: Maney, 2007).

Jacoby, F., *Das marmor Parium, herausgegeben und erklärt* (Berlin: Weidmann, 1904).

_____ , *Die Fragmente der griechischen Historiker*, II B (Leiden: Brill reprint, 1997); Kommentar II B (Leiden: Brill reprint, 1993).

Jameson, M. H., D. R. Jordan, and R. D. Kotansky, *A Lex Sacra from Selinous* (Greek, Roman, and Byzantine Monographs 11; Durham, NC: Duke University, 1993).

Johnson, W., "Greek Electronic Resources and the Lexicographical Function," in *Biblical Greek Language and Lexicography: Essays in Honor of Frederick W. Danker* (ed. B. Taylor, J. Lee, P. Burton, and R. Whitaker; Grand Rapids, MI: Eerdmans, 2004), 75–84.

Jones, C. P., "Two Epigrams from Nicomedia and Its Region," *ZPE* 21 (1976): 189–91.

Joosten, J., "The Historical and Theological Lexicon of the Septuagint: A Sample Entry—εὐλογέω," in *XIV Congress of the IOSCS, Helsinki, 2010* (ed. M. K. H. Peters; SBLSCS 59; Atlanta: SBL, 2013), 347–55.

_____ , "Le milieu producteur du Pentateuque grec," *REJ* 165 (2006): 349–61.

_____ , "The Septuagint as a Source of Information on Egyptian Aramaic in the Hellenistic Period," in *Aramaic in Its Historical and Linguistic Setting* (ed. H. Gzella and M. L. Folmer; Veröffentlichungen der Orientalistischen Kommission 50; Wiesbaden: Harrassowitz, 2008), 93–105.

_____ , "To See God. Conflicting Exegetical Tendencies in the Septuagint," in *Die Septuaginta – Texte, Kontexte, Lebenswelten* (ed. M. Karrer and W. Kraus; WUNT 219; Tübingen: Mohr Siebeck, 2008), 287–99.

_____ , "Le vocabulaire de la Septante et la question du sociolecte des juifs alexandrins: Le cas du verbe εὐλογέω, «bénir»," in *Septuagint Vocabulary: Pre-History, Usage, Reception* (ed. E. Bons and J. Joosten; SBLSCS 58; Atlanta: SBL, 2011), 13–23.

Kloner, A., "Maresha in the Reign of Ptolemy II Philadelphus," in *Ptolemy the Second Philadelphus and His World* (ed. P. R. McKechnie and P. Guillaume; Leiden: Brill, 2008), 171–82.

Kooij, A. van der, "On the Place of Origin of the Old Greek of Psalms," *VT* 33 (1983): 67–74.

Kraft, R. A., ed., *Septuagintal Lexicography* (SBLSCS 1; Missoula, MT: Society of Biblical Literature, 1972).

Kreissig, H., *Wirtschaft und Gesellschaft im Seleukidenreich: die Eigentums- und die Abhängigkeitsverhältnisse* (Schriften zur Geschichte und Kultur der Antike 16; Berlin: Akademie-Verlag, 1978).

Laks, A., and G. W. Most, eds., *Studies on the Derveni Papyrus* (Oxford: Oxford University Press, 1997).

Lane, E. N., "Παστός," *Glotta* 66 (1988): 100–23.

Larcher, C., *Le livre de la sagesse, ou, La sagesse de Salomon* (Paris: Gabalda, 1983–85).

Laronde, A., "Huios tès poléôs," in *Cyrène à Catherine. Trois mille ans de Libyennes. Études grecques et latines offertes à Catherine Dobias Lalou* (ed. F. Poli and G. Vottéro; Nancy: A.D.R.A., 2005), 149–59.

Le Boullec, A., and P. Sandevoir, *L'Exode* (La Bible d'Alexandrie 2; Paris: Cerf, 1989).

Lee, J. A. L., "Equivocal and Stereotyped Renderings in the LXX," *RB* 87 (1980): 104–17.

_____ , *A History of New Testament Lexicography* (Studies in Biblical Greek 8; New York: Peter Lang, 2003).

_____ , *A Lexical Study of the Septuagint Version of the Pentateuch* (SBLSCS 14; Chico, CA: Scholars, 1983).

_____ , "*A Lexical Study* Thirty Years On, with Observations on 'Order' Words in the LXX Pentateuch," in *Emanuel: Studies in Hebrew Bible, Septuagint and Dead Sea Scrolls in Honor of Emanuel Tov* (ed. S. M. Paul, R. A. Kraft, L. H. Schiffman, and W. W. Fields; VTSup 94; Leiden: Brill, 2003), 513–24.

_____ , "A Note on Septuagint Material in the Supplement to Liddell and Scott," *Glotta* 47 (1969): 234–42.

_____ , "The Present State of Lexicography of Ancient Greek," in *Biblical Greek Language and Lexicography: Essays in Honor of Frederick W. Danker* (ed. B. Taylor, J. Lee, P. Burton, and R. Whitaker; Grand Rapids, MI: Eerdmans, 2004), 66–74.

_____ , "Releasing Liddell-Scott-Jones from Its Past," in *Classical Dictionaries: Past, Present and Future* (ed. Christopher Stray; London: Duckworth 2010), 119–38.

_____ , "Some Features of the Speech of Jesus in Mark's Gospel," *NovT* 27 (1985): 1–26.

_____ , "The Vocabulary of the Septuagint and Documentary Evidence," in *Handbuch zur Septuaginta: IV Sprache* (ed. E. Bons and J. Joosten; Gütersloh: Gütersloher Verlagshaus), forthcoming.

_____ , "ἐξαποστέλλω," in *Voces Biblicae: Septuagint Greek and Its Significance for the New Testament* (ed. Jan Joosten and Peter J. Tomson; CBET 49; Leuven: Peeters, 2007), 99–113.

Lincicum, D. C., "Greek Deuteronomy's 'Fever and Chills' and Their Magical Afterlife," *VT* 58 (2008): 544–49.

_____ , "The Epigraphic Habit and the Biblical Text: Inscriptions as a Source for the Study of the Greek Bible," *BIOSCS* 41 (2008): 84–92.

Lust, J., "J. F. Schleusner and the Lexicon of the Septuagint," *ZAW* 102 (1990): 256–62.

_____ , "Two New Lexica of the Septuagint and Related Examples," *JNSL* 19 (1993): 95–105.

Lust, J., E. Eynikel, and K. Hauspie, eds., *A Greek–English Lexicon of the Septuagint, Revised Edition* (Stuttgart: Deutsche Bibelgesellschaft, 2003).

Mahaffy, J. P., *The Flinders Petrie Papyri: With Transcriptions, Commentaries and Index* (3 vols.; Dublin: Academy House, 1893).

Mainardi, M., "Il culto di Atena a Mesambria Pontica," in *Culti e miti greci in aree periferiche* (ed. T. Alfieri Tonini, G. Bagnasco Gianni, and F. Cordano; Aristonothos, Scritti per il Mediterraneo antico 6; Trento: Tangram Edizioni Scientifiche, 2012), 177–204.

Maiuri, A., *Herculaneum and the Villa of the Papyri* (Novara: Instituto Geografico de Agostini, 1963).

Mardaga, H., "Hapax Legomena and the Idiolect of John," *NovT* 56 (2014): 134–53.

Mathieson, E. A., "The Language of the Gospels: Evidence from the Inscriptions and the Papyri," in *The Content and the Setting of the Gospel Tradition* (ed. M. Harding and A. Nobbs; Grand Rapids, MI: Eerdmans, 2010), 62–78.

McLean, B. H., *An Introduction to Greek Epigraphy of the Hellenistic and Roman Periods from Alexander the Great down to the Reign of Constantine (323 B.C.–A.D. 337)* (Ann Arbor, MI: University of Michigan Press, 2002).

Meadows, A., "Ptolemaic Possessions outside Egypt," in *The Encyclopedia of Ancient History* (ed. R. S. Bagnall, K. Brodersen, C. B. Champion, A. Erskine, and S. R. Huebner; London: Blackwell, 2013), 5625–29.

Meer, M. N. van der, "Problems and Perspectives in Septuagint Lexicography: The Case of Non-Compliance (ΑΠΕΙΘΕΩ)," in *Septuagint Vocabulary: Pre-History, Usage, Reception* (ed. J. Joosten and E. Bons; Atlanta: SBL, 2011), 65–86.

————, "Trendy Translations in the Septuagint of Isaiah: A Study of the Vocabulary of the Greek Isaiah 3,18–23 in the Light of Contemporary Sources," in *Die Septuaginta—Texte, Kontexte, Lebenswelten. Internationale Fachtagung veranstaltet von Septuaginta Deutsch (LXX.D), Wuppertal 20.-23. Juli 2006* (ed. M. Karrer und W. Kraus; WUNT 252; Tübingen: Mohr Siebeck, 2008), 581–96.

Meiggs, R., and D. M. Lewis, *Greek Historical Inscriptions* (rev. ed.; Oxford: Oxford University Press, 1988).

Merkelbach, R., and J. Stauber, *Jenseits des Euphrat: griechische Inschriften. Ein epigraphisches Lesebuch. Zusammengestellt, übersetzt und erklärt* (Munich: Saur, 2005).

Meyboom, P. G. P., *The Nile Mosaic of Palestrina: Early Evidence of Egyptian Religion in Italy* (Leiden: Brill, 1995).

Mihailov, G., ed., *Inscriptiones graecae in Bulgaria repertae, Vol. 1: Inscriptiones orae Ponti Euxini* (2nd ed.; Sofia: In aedibus typographicis Academiae Litterarum Bulgaricae, 1970).

Millar, F., "Epigraphy," in *Sources for Ancient History* (ed. M. Crawford, E. Gabba, F. Millar, and A. M. Snodgrass; Cambridge: Cambridge University Press, 1983), 80–136.

Milne, J. G., *Greek Inscriptions* (Service des Antiquités de l'Égypte: Catalogue géneral des antiquités égyptiennes du Musée du Caire; Oxford: Oxford University Press, 1905).

Mitford, T. B., "The Hellenistic Inscriptions of Old Paphos," *ABSA* 56 (1961): 1–41.

Moffitt, D. M., and C. J. Butera, "P.Duk.Inv. 727: A Dispute with 'Proselytes' in Egypt," *ZPE* 177 (2011): 201–6.

Moffitt, J. F., "The Palestrina Mosaic with a 'Nile Scene': Philostratus and Ekphrasis; Ptolemy and Chorographia," *Zeitschrift für Kunstgeschichte* 60 (1997): 227–47.

Montevecchi, O., "Quaedam de graecitate psalmorum cum papyris comparata," in *Proceedings of the IX International Congress of Papyrology. Oslo 19–22 August 1958* (Oslo: Norwegian Universities Press, 1963), 293–310. Reprinted in *Bibbia e papiri: luce dai papiri sulla Bibbia greca, a cura di A. Passoni Dell'Acqua* (Estudis de papirologia i filologia bíblica 5; Barcelona: Institut de Teologia Fondamental, Seminari de Papirologia, 1999), 97–120.

Morgan, T., *Literate Education in the Hellenistic and Roman Worlds* (Cambridge Classical Studies; Cambridge: Cambridge University Press, 1998), 219–26.

Moulton, J. H., *From Egyptian Rubbish-Heaps: Five Popular Lectures on the New Testament* (London: Charles H. Kelly, 1916).

_____, "The Science of Language and the Study of the NT," in *The Christian Religion in the Study and in the Street* (London: Hodder and Stoughton, 1919), 117–44.

Moulton, J. H., and G. Milligan, *The Vocabulary of the Greek Testament Illustrated from the Papyri and Other Non-Literary Sources* (8 fascicles; London: Hodder and Stoughton, 1914–29).

Muraoka, T., *A Greek–English Lexicon of the Septuagint* (Leuven: Peeters, 2009).

_____, *A Greek–Hebrew/Aramaic Two-Way Index to the Septuagint* (Leuven: Peeters, 2010).

Oster, R., "The Ephesian Artemis 'Whom All Asia and the World Worship' (Acts 19:27): Representative Epigraphical Testimony to Ἄρτεμις Ἐφεσία Outside Ephesos," in *Transmission and Reception: New Testament Text-Critical and Exegetical Studies* (ed. D. C. Parker; Texts and Studies. Third Series 4; Piscataway, NJ: Gorgias, 2006), 212–31.

Passoni Dell'Acqua, A., "Contributi alla lessicografia dei LXX. I nuovi lessici. In margine a T. Muraoka, *A Greek-English Lexicon of the Septuagint,*" *Aegyptus* 74 (1994): 129–35.

_____, "Il Pentateuco dei LXX testimone di istituzioni di età tolemaica," *Annali di Scienze religiose* 4 (1999): 171–200.

_____, "La terminologia dei reati nei προστάγματα dei Tolemei e nella versione dei LXX," in *Proceedings of the XVIIIth International Congress of Papyrology, Athens 25–31 May 1986* (ed. B. G. Mandilaras; 2 vols.; Athens: Greek Papyrological Society, 1988), 2: 335–50.

Passow, F., *Handwörterbuch der griechischen Sprache* (2 vols; 4th ed.; Leipzig: Vogel, 1831).

_____, *Wörterbuch der griechischen Sprache, Völlig neu bearb. Wilhelm Crönert* (Göttingen: Vandenhoeck and Ruprecht, 1913).

Peek, W., *Attische Versinschriften* (ASAW 69.2; Berlin: Akademie-Verlag, 1980).

_____, *Griechische Vers-Inschriften, 1. Grab-Epigramme* (Berlin: Akademie-Verlag, 1955).

_____, "Milesische Versinschriften," *ZPE* 7 (1971): 193–226.

Peters, J. P., and H. Thiersch, *Painted Tombs in the Necropolis of Marissa (Marēshah)* (ed. S. A. Cook; London: Committee of the Palestine Exploration Fund, 1905).

Pietersma, A., "The Place of Origin of the Old Greek Psalter," in *The World of the Aramaeans I: Biblical Studies in Honour of Paul-Eugène Dion* (JSOTSup 324; ed. P. M. Michèle Daviau, J. W. Wevers, and M. Weigl; Sheffield: Sheffield Academic, 2001), 252–74.

Piper, O. A., "New Testament Lexicography: An Unfinished Task," *Festschrift to Honor F. Wilbur Gingrich: Lexicographer, Scholar, Teacher, and Committed Christian Layman* (ed. E. H. Barth and R. E. Cocroft; Leiden: Brill, 1972), 177–204.

Pleket, H. W., "Religious History as the History of Mentality: The 'Believer' as Servant of the Deity in the Greek World," in *Faith, Hope and Worship: Aspects of Religious Mentality in the Ancient World* (ed. H. S. Versnel; Leiden: Brill, 1981), 152–92.

Porter, S. E., ed., *Diglossia and Other Topics in New Testament Linguistics* (Sheffield: Sheffield Academic, 2000).

————, *Studies in the Greek New Testament: Theory and Practice* (New York: Peter Lang, 1996).

Preisigke, F., and E. Kiessling, *Wörterbuch der griechischen Papyrusurkunden mit Einschluss der griechischen Inschriften, Ausschriften, Ostraka, Mumienschilder usw. aus Ägypten* (4 vols.; Berlin: Selbstverlag der Erben, 1924–44).

Procksch, O., "ἅγιος, etc.," in *Theologisches Wörterbuch zum Neuen Testament* (ed. G. Kittel and G. Friedrich; 11 vols.; Stuttgart: Kohlhammer, 1932–79), 1: 87–116.

Rehkopf, F., *Septuaginta-Vokabular* (Göttingen: Vandenhoeck & Ruprecht, 1989).

Rehm, A., *Didyma II: Die Inschriften* (Berlin: Mann, 1958).

Renehan, R., *Greek Lexicographical Notes: A Critical Supplement to the Greek-English Lexicon of Liddell-Scott-Jones* (Hypomnemata 45; Göttingen: Vandenhoeck & Ruprecht, 1975).

————, *Greek Lexicographical Notes: A Critical Supplement to the Greek-English Lexicon of Liddell-Scott-Jones. Series 2* (Hypomnemata 74; Göttingen: Vandenhoeck & Ruprecht, 1982).

Reynolds, J. M., *Aphrodisias and Rome: Documents from the Excavation of the Theatre at Aphrodisias Conducted by Kenan T. Erim, Together with Some Related Texts* (Journal of Roman Studies Monograph 1; London: Society for the Promotion of Roman Studies, 1982).

Robert, L., "Malédictions funéraires grecques," *Comptes rendus des séances de l'Académie des Inscriptions et Belles-Lettres* 122 (1978): 241–89.

————, *Le sanctuaire de Sinuri près de Mylasa, I. Les inscriptions* (Mémoires de l'Institut français d'archéologie de Stamboul 7; Paris: de Boccard, 1945).

Rodríguez Somolinos, H., "El DGE y la epigrafía griega: el problema de las palabras fantasma (ejemplificación y tipología)," in *La lexicografía griega y el Diccionario Griego-Español, DGE. Anejo VI* (ed. F. R. Adrados and J. Rodríguez Somolinos; Madrid: CSIC, 2005), 165–75.

Şahin, S., "Neue Inschriften von der bithynischen Halbinsel," *ZPE* 18 (1975): 27–48.

Scarpat, G., *Libro della Sapienza: testo, traduzione, introduzione e commento* (3 vols.; Brescia: Paideia, 1989–99).

Schleusner, J. F., *Novum Lexicon graeco-latinum in Novum Testamentum: congessit et variis observationibus philologicis illustravit* (2 vols.; Lepizig: in officina Weidmanniana, 1792).

_____ , *Novus thesaurus philologico-criticus, sive lexicon in lxx et reliquos interpretes graecos ac scriptores apocryphos veteris testamenti* (5 vols.; Leipzig: in libraria Weidmannia, 1820 21).

Schoors, A., *The Preacher Sought to Find Pleasing Words: A Study of the Language of Qoheleth* (2 vols.; Leuven: Peeters, 1992–2004).

Searles, H. M., *A Lexicographical Study of the Greek Inscriptions* (Studies in Classical Philology 2; Chicago: University of Chicago Press, 1899).

Seeligman, I. L., *The Septuagint Version of Isaiah: A Discussion of Its Problems* (Mededelingen en verhandelingen van het Vooraziatisch-Egyptisch Genootschap "Ex Oriente Lux" 9. Leiden: Brill, 1948).

Shaw, F., "Review of T. Muraoka, *A Greek–English Lexicon of the Septuagint*," *Bryn Mawr Classical Review* 2010.04.20 [online: bmcr.brynmawr. edu/2010/2010-04-20.html].

Sider, D., *The Library of the Villa dei Papiri at Herculaneum* (Los Angeles: J. Paul Getty Museum, 2005).

Silva, M., "Bilingualism and the Character of Palestinian Greek," *Bib* 61 (1980): 198–219.

Smith, M. F., *The Philosophical Inscription of Diogenes of Oinoanda* (Vienna: Verlag der Österreichischen Akademie der Wissenschaften, 1996).

Sokolowski, F., *Lois sacrées des cités grecques* (Travaux et mémoires 18; Paris: de Boccard, 1969).

Sollamo, R., "Some 'Improper' Prepositions, Such as ΕΝΩΠΙΟΝ, ΕΝΑΝΤΙΟΝ, ΕΝΑΝΤΙ, Etc., in the Septuagint and Early Koine Greek," *VT* 25 (1975): 773–82.

Souza, P. de, *Piracy in the Graeco-Roman World* (Cambridge: Cambridge University Press, 1999).

Stenhouse, W., *Reading Inscriptions and Writing Ancient History: Historical Scholarship in the Late Renaissance* (Bulletin of the Institute of Classical Studies Supplement 86; London: Institute of Classical Studies, 2005).

Stricker, B. H., "Trois études de phonétique et de morphologie coptes," *AcOr* 15 (1937): 1–20.

Swete, H. B., *An Introduction to the Old Testament in Greek with an Appendix Containing the Letter of Aristeas Edited by H. St. J. Thackeray* (rev. R. R. Ottley; Cambridge: Cambridge University Press, 1914).

Talshir, Z., *I Esdras: A Text Critical Commentary* (SBLSCS 50; Atlanta: Society of Biblical Literature, 2001).

_____, *I Esdras: From Origin to Translation* (SBLSCS 47; Atlanta: Society of Biblical Literature, 1999).

Taylor, B. A., *The Analytical Lexicon to the Septuagint: A Complete Parsing Guide* (Grand Rapids, MI: Zondervan, 1994; 2nd ed., 2010).

Teodorsson, S.-T., "Phonological Variation in Classical Attic and the Development of Koine," *Glotta* 57 (1979): 61–75.

Thackeray, H. St. J., *A Grammar of the Old Testament in Greek according to the Septuagint, Vol. 1: Introduction, Orthography and Accidence* (Cambridge: Cambridge University Press, 1909).

Thiersch, H. G. J., *De Pentateuchi versione Alexandrina: libri tres* (Erlangae: apud Theod. Blaesing, 1841).

Threatte, L., *The Grammar of Attic Inscriptions* (2 vols.; Berlin: de Gruyter, 1980–96).

Tov, E., "The 'Lucianic' Text of the Canonical and the Apocryphal Sections of Esther: A Rewritten Biblical Book" (revised version), in E. Tov, *The Greek and Hebrew Bible: Collected Essays on the Septuagint* (VTSup 72; Leiden: Brill, 1999), 535–48.

_____, "Reflections on the Septuagint with Special Attention Paid to the Post-Pentateuchal Translations," in *Die Septuaginta—Texte, Theologien, Einflüsse. 2. Internationale Fachtagung veranstaltet von Septuaginta Deutsch (LXX.D), Wuppertal 23.–27. Juli 2008* (ed. W. Kraus, M. Karrer, and M. Meiser; WUNT 252; Tubingen: Mohr Siebeck, 2010), 3–22.

_____, "Some Thoughts on a Lexicon of a Septuagint," in E. Tov, *The Greek and Hebrew Bible: Collected Essays on the Septuagint* (VTSup 72; Leiden: Brill, 1999), 97–108.

Traversa, A., "Iscrizione metrica da Alessandria," *Aegyptus* 35 (1955): 137–38.

_____, "L'iscrizione metrica per Felice," in Ἀντίδωρον *Hugoni Henrico Paoli oblatum: Miscellanea philologica* (Pubblicazioni dell'Istituto di filologia classica 8; Genoa: Istituto di filologia classica, 1956), 283–322.

_____, "Replica a una 'postilla,'" *Epigraphica* 17 (1955): 15–32.

Treat, J. C., "Aquila, Field, and the Song of Songs," in *Origen's Hexapla and Fragments. Papers Presented at the Rich Seminar on the Hexapla, Oxford Centre for Hebrew and Jewish Studies, 25th [July]–3rd August 1994* (ed. A. Salvesen; TSAJ 58; Tübingen: Mohr Siebeck, 1998), 135–76.

Turner, E. G., *Greek Papyri: An Introduction* (Oxford: Clarendon, 1980).

Vanderlip, V. F., *The Four Greek Hymns of Isidorus and the Cult of Isis* (American Studies in Papyrology 12; Toronto: Hakkert, 1972).

Vattioni, F., "La lessicografia dei LXX nei papiri," *Studia Papyrologica* 19 (1980): 39–59.

Venetz, H.-J., *Quinta des Psalteriums: ein Beitrag zur Septuaginta- und Hexaplaforschung* (Collection Massorah 1; Études classiques et texts 2; Hildesheim: Gerstenberg, 1974).

Wackernagel, J., *Hellenistica* (Göttingen: Kaestner, 1907).

Walch, J. E. I., *Observationes in Matthaeum ex graecis inscriptionibus* (Jena: apud Vam J. R. Croeckeri, 1779).

Weisshäupl, R., "Ephesische Latrinen-Inschriften," *JÖAI* 5 Beiblatt (1902): 33–34.

Welles, C. B., *Royal Correspondence in the Hellenistic Period: A Study in Greek Epigraphy* (New Haven: Yale University Press, 1934).

White, J. L., *Light from Ancient Letters* (Foundations and Facets; Philadelphia: Fortress, 1986).

Wilhelm, A., "Bemerkungen zu den attischen Grabinschriften I.G.II²," *ZPE* 29 (1978): 57–90.

Williams, C., "Hellenistic and Roman Buildings in the Mediaeval Walls of Mytilene," *Phoenix* 38 (1984): 31–76.

Winston, D., *The Wisdom of Solomon: A New Translation with Introduction and Commentary* (AB 43; Garden City, NY: Doubleday, 1979).

Wright, B. G., "The Letter of Aristeas and the Question of Septuagint Origins Redux," *Journal of Ancient Judaism* 2 (2011): 303–25.

————, "Δοῦλος and Παῖς as Translations of עבד: Lexical Equivalences and Conceptual Transformations," in *IX Congress of the International Organization for Septuagint and Cognate Studies. Cambridge, 1995* (ed. B. A. Taylor; SBLSCS 45; Atlanta: Scholars, 1997), 263–77.

Xuefu, D., "Neologismus und Neologismenwörterbuch," in *Wörterbücher in der Diskussion: Vorträge aus dem Heidelberger Lexikographischen Kolloquium* (ed. H. E. Wiegand; Lexicographica. Series maior 27; Tübingen: Niemeyer, 1989), 39–73.

Zuntz, G., "Aristeas Studies II: Aristeas on the Translation of the Torah," *JSS* 4 (1959): 109–26.

Index of Modern Authors

Index of Ancient Authors and Sources

Index of Scripture

Septuagint

New Testament

Index of Inscriptions

Index of Papyri

Index of Words

Aramaic

Demotic

Greek

Hebrew

2014. 11. 13   28.95 (26.00)